The Cultural World of Jesus
Sunday by Sunday
Cycle C

John J. Pilch

A Liturgical Press Book

THE LITURGICAL PRESS
Collegeville, Minnesota

Cover design by David Manahan, O.S.B. Photo courtesy of Hugh Witzmann, O.S.B.

1   2   3   4   5   6   7   8

Library of Congress Cataloging-in-Publication Data

Pilch, John J.
    The cultural world of Jesus : Sunday by Sunday / John J. Pilch.
        p.   cm.
    Includes bibliographical references.
    Contents: [1] Cycle C
    ISBN 0-8146-2288-7 (cycle C)
    1. Bible   N. T.   Gospels–Liturgical lessons, English.   2. Bible.
N. T.   Gospels–Meditations.   3. Bible.   N. T.   Gospels–History
of Biblical events.   4. Middle East–Civilization.   I. Title.
BX2170.C55P49   1997
264'.34–dc20   94-44772
                                                                CIP

For Sylvester Makarewicz, O.F.M.,
Dacian Bluma, O.F.M.,
Edgar Śmigiel, O.F.M.,
all the Friars of Assumption Province (U.S.A.),
and all my Franciscan friends who
"made known to me the fragrant words of the Lord"
(Francis of Assisi, Letter to all the Faithful)

Contents

Introduction

The idea for these reflections from a Mediterranean cultural perspective on the gospel read at Sunday liturgies originated in a monthly column I wrote for *Modern Liturgy* over a two-year period (1989–91). When my tenure as columnist ended, I persuaded Initiatives Professional Speaker Registry to publish a brief weekly reflection on a subscription basis. This one-page bulletin-insert quickly became very popular with adult enrichment and RCIA groups. I have been delighted when visiting parishes to conduct Bible study seminars to see parishioners diligently reading the insert and checking the missalette before Mass.

It has been even more satisfying to hear the preacher say: "My topic this morning is x. Other interesting ideas about today's gospel can be found in the bulletin insert. I encourage you to read and reflect on that page with your Bible at home. For this morning, however, let us reflect on my topic, x." Often the preacher further develops a topic from the insert and makes significantly appropriate applications to the local community.

This collection of reflections is revised and slightly larger than the subscription series. The architects of the lectionary have provided readings for fifty-six Sundays in each year's cycle. No liturgical year lasts fifty-six weeks. Lent, Easter, and other feasts cause various Sundays to be omitted each year. This collection treats only the gospels assigned for the fifty-six Sundays as found in the lectionary. It does not include the gospels for feasts that sometimes fall on a Sunday.

The *Interpretation of the Bible in the Church,* published in 1993 by the Pontifical Biblical Commission, highlighted some distinctive insights that Mediterranean cultural anthropology can shed on interpreting the Bible. The concepts presented in that document reflect the publications of The Context Group, an association of biblical scholars of which I am a charter member. For nearly two decades this group has dedicated itself to studying the Mediterranean backgrounds of the New Testament. The Biblical Commission's document presents concepts developed in research papers read by Context Group members at a scientific meeting in Spain in 1991. The list of recommended readings that concludes this volume identifies some of these ground-breaking studies whose insights are liberally reflected in my reflections.

I have not listed the excellent gospel commentaries and commentaries on the lectionary that adopt other approaches and are readily available for anyone desiring a more comprehensive treatment of these texts. The focus here is exclusively on the Mediterranean cultural perspective.

Purists or sensates on the Myers-Briggs scale may object to the global adjective "Mediterranean." They will correctly insist on recognizing the differences of each country in this part of the world. Nevertheless, reputable specialists in Mediterranean culture convincingly demonstrate that this region (which they sometimes call "Circum-Mediterranean"—see George Foster, *Culture and Conquest* [Chicago: Quadrangle Books, 1960] p. 25) shares many cultural elements in common, unchanged over several millennia. The core values of honor and shame are two such basic elements. Details of honorable and shameful behavior do indeed differ from country to country, but the global concept is still helpful as a safeguard against ethnocentrism. These reflections present the characteristics of the first-century Eastern Mediterranean region.

Thus I use the words "Mediterranean" or "Middle-Eastern" to describe the culture of the people who populate and whose lives are reflected in the pages of the Bible. Insights about the culture of this world are derived from contemporary anthropological investigations, particularly the research of Mediterranean anthropologists such as Leila Abu-Lughod, Camillia Fawzi El-Solh, Soraya Altorki, Elizabeth Warnock Fernea, David Gilmore, and members of The Context Group.

Anthropologists agree that the judicious use of contemporary data, tied to historical accounts, is basic and reliable anthropological methodology (see Foster, *Culture and Conquest*, p. 30). It is legitimate anthropological method to retroject contemporary insights over two and three thousand years because until the advent of colonialism and the discovery of oil and its consequences, the culture of the Mediterranean region remained remarkably unchanged.

These reflections, then, attempt to fulfill the exhortations of the Second Vatican Council, which urged interpreters of the Bible to pay due attention to the "characteristic styles of perceiving" that prevailed at the time of the sacred author (Dogmatic Constitution on Divine Revelation, 12). Perception is governed by culture. The better an interpreter knows the culture in which the Bible originated, the more culturally plausible will be the interpretation.

It is precisely this understanding that stands behind the instruction for preachers that cautions: "When they narrate biblical events, let them not add imaginative details which are not consonant with the truth" (The 1964 Instruction on the Historical Truth of the Gospels, par. 13). The phrase "consonant with the truth" is best rendered "culturally plausible."

Moreover, *The Interpretation of the Bible in the Church* urges preachers to focus on the central contribution of lectionary texts in order to actualize and inculturate the text appropriately in the lives of the listeners. The approach of cultural anthropology is admirably suited to helping achieve this goal in the liturgy.

Preachers are fond of quoting the literal Greek translation from John's Gospel, that Jesus "became human and pitched his tent among us" (1:14). Specifically and in the concrete, Jesus was a first-century, Middle-Eastern peasant, driven by the core cultural values of honor and shame, expert in the art of challenge and riposte, and master of all his culture's strategies. From a historical perspective, Jesus was neither a

Jew nor a Christian, since these identities did not exist in the first century. The identity and term "Jew" as we understand it today is rooted in the Talmud of the fourth and fifth century of the common era, while the identity and term "Christian" is the result of the christological debates of the first three or four centuries of the common era.

Historically, Jesus belongs to the period of Second-Temple Judaism, and the appropriate "in-group" term is "Israel/Israelite" (see Luke 7:9; 24:21) or member of the house of Israel, while the common "out-group" term for these people is "Judean" (Luke 23:3), often incorrectly translated "Jew." The term "Christian" appears only four times in the New Testament. It is never a self-designation. This is what others call those who believe in Jesus Messiah (Acts 11:26). In some instances is it definitely a derogatory term (Acts 26:28; 1 Pet 4:16-17).

The end result of this historically and culturally precise insight is that in all three volumes of this series, unless the reference is to modern times, the words Jew/Jewish and Christian do not appear. In speaking of the ancient world, these volumes have referred to Judeans or Judaic traditions, or Messianists and Messianist interpretations. Those who followed and believed in Jesus in his day and after he died and was raised believed him to be the chosen and anointed one (Messiah) of God.

The challenge to Western believers is to understand and appreciate Jesus on his own terms with historical accuracy and cultural respect. To this I hope my reflections make some modest contribution.

Feast of St. Anthony of Padua   John J. Pilch
June 13, 1997   Georgetown University

First Sunday of Advent
Luke 21:25-28, 34-36

Like all the evangelists, Luke also consulted sources in writing his Gospel. He admits this in his introduction (Luke 1:1-4). Scholars generally agree that Mark, the earliest written Gospel, was one of these sources. Today's reading, which is extracted from Luke 21, is itself based on Mark 13. Many modern believers think these chapters describe the end of the world. In a certain sense they do, but this is intertwined with information about the destruction of the Jerusalem Temple in A.D. 70. When Mark wrote, this event had not yet taken place. When Luke wrote (about A.D. 85), this had already happened.

What, then, does Luke want to tell his readers now that the Temple no longer exists? The verses selected for today's liturgy highlight that part of the tradition.

In verses 25–28, Luke separates "what is coming upon the world" (v. 26, a future event) from what has already come upon Jerusalem (a past event in Luke's day). The judgment that will take place at the "coming of the Son of Man on a cloud" (v. 27) will be far more important and far greater than the judgment on the Jerusalem Temple that followed upon its rejection of Jesus as teacher. Here Luke sounds a clear warning for his readers.

Faithful believers, however, have nothing to fear. When they see the cosmic signs and the earthly catastrophes that strike terror in others, they should know that their personal rescue or deliverance is near. Translations that speak of

1

"redemption" in this verse do not refer to Christ's death and resurrection but rather rescue from this impending distress. Whence such confidence? Luke gives his explanation in verses 34–36. This advice may derive from Luke's special source, "L," that is, materials unknown by the other evangelists. Or it may even be Luke's personal creation. Whatever the source of these verses, Luke remains consistent with his exhortation to vigilance and prayer.

VIGILANCE

In particular he cautions against carousing, drunkenness, and worldly cares (v. 34), which weigh a person down and distract from pressing issues. Americans may snicker at this trio of distractions and conclude that our ancestors in the Faith were not very different from us. That would be a serious mistake.

The ordinary peasants, who constituted about 95 percent of the population of first-century Palestine, lived at a subsistence level and would hardly have the means or the opportunity to carouse, to get drunk, or to dream about and pursue creature comforts. They regularly worried about where the next meal was coming from and whether there would be enough for everyone. In other words, they were intensely focused on the present moment and the challenge of staying alive.

No, this kind of warning would be directed particularly to the elites, who had both the leisure and opportunity to carouse and get drunk and to allow themselves to be consumed by "worldly cares." Luke addresses especially the wealthy who are greedy, who refuse to share (see Luke 12:13-34, esp. v. 15) with the needy, as this culture honorably requires. Indeed, at every mention of the "rich" in Luke's Gospel it is advisable to cross out that word and pencil in "greedy." That is what irks Luke and Luke's Jesus and, indeed, all the people of Luke's Gospel.

Such people will be caught quite by surprise when the Son of Man returns in judgment! No wonder Luke urges: "Keep yourselves awake."

PRAYER

Religious prayer is a form of communication directed to a person who is perceived as controlling the general order of existence. In the Bible, this is God. The cosmic signs and earthly catastrophes that Luke has described are clearly under God's control. Hence while Americans would be prone to check with their intelligence-gathering and weather satellites, radio telescopes, astronomers, meteorologists, or the CIA to identify and evaluate cosmic signs and imminent earthly catastrophes, Luke's advice to believers is to "pray [to God] that you may be strong enough to escape from all these things."

Our ancestors in the Faith who were the first to hear or read Luke's warnings were mired down in present concerns. Peasants fought to survive; the elite sought to make life even more elite. Americans tend to think so much about the future that they totally miss the present. Digital wristwatches remind all of us of how fleeting the present moment is. The advice of Luke's Jesus suits listeners of every era: "Keep awake!" so that you can escape the final calamity.

Second Sunday of Advent
Luke 3:1-6

Roughly speaking, between 150 B.C. and A.D. 250 a general "baptist" movement existed in Palestine. Numerous Judaic and Messianist groups at this time practiced some kind of ritual washing, or baptism. These groups included the Essenes at Qumran, the Ebionites, John and his disciples, Jesus and his disciples (see John 3:25; 4:1), and a variety of Gnostic believers.

John the Baptist and his group were very well known. When Herod Antipas heard about the ministry of Jesus, he expressed an opinion common at that time that John the Baptist had risen from the dead. "John I beheaded; but who is this about whom I hear such things?" (Luke 9:7-9).

Moreover, John the Baptist made many converts and had many followers. In Acts of the Apostles, the companion volume to his Gospel, Luke notes that in Ephesus Priscilla and Aquila recognized Apollos as a disciple baptized by John (Acts 18:25). Though Apollos knew and taught things about Jesus accurately, they explained things to him even "more accurately" (18:26). Paul, too, found twelve additional disciples in Ephesus baptized by John (Acts 19:1-7) and rebaptized them in the name of Jesus.

The baptisms administered by these various groups took different forms and had diverse meanings attached to them. Luke explains John's baptism thus: "a baptism of repentance for the forgiveness of sins."

4

REPENTANCE

The heart of the Baptizer's message is the need for repentance. The Greek word and its Hebrew counterpart were very familiar to his listeners. In ordinary daily life the words meant simply "a change of mind." In a religious context the same words took on the meaning of "broadening of horizons, transformation of experience, reform of life." We commonly use the word "conversion."

In the Judaic mind the religious sense of these words included the idea of "turning" to God from ways that are disobedient or displeasing. In exhorting the prophet Ezekiel to be a faithful preacher, God says: "If you warn the wicked, and they *do not turn* from their wickedness or their wicked way, they shall die for their iniquity" (Ezek 3:19). Clearly a human effort is demanded: a personal taking stock and a resolution to do something about what one discovers.

FORGIVENESS OF SINS

Turning to God will obtain forgiveness of sins. The Baptizer does not explain his meaning, but in the Gospels, the closest analogy for this phrase is "forgiveness of debts." This, in fact, is what Luke writes in his version of the Lord's Prayer: "forgive us our sins for we too forgive everyone who is indebted to us" (Luke 11:4; cf. Matt 6:12). Here, sin is the same as debt.

Peasants are very familiar with debt. They live in debt all the time. In the peasant world of first-century Palestine debt threatened the loss of land, livelihood, and family. Recall Jesus' parable in Matthew 18:23-25 where the man who could not pay the ten thousand talents he owed was ordered to be sold together with his wife and children and all his possessions so that the debt could be collected.

That peasant succeeded in begging forgiveness from the king (v. 27). He managed to save his life and his honor. Unfortunately, he did not reciprocate to a fellow peasant who owed him far less. In the end, the king commanded this ungrateful wretch "to be tortured" until he would pay his entire debt (v. 34).

In today's gospel reading, the Baptizer is urging his listeners to turn to God from their wicked ways so that God would forgive and forget what was owed. For John the ritual of washing in the Jordan symbolized this turning. Though the specific meaning of John's ritual washing is never explicitly explained in the Gospels, a similar practice at Qumran provides a plausible background.

In the Qumran *Rule of the Community* (5:13-14) we read: "They [prospective members of the community] shall not enter the water [in order] to share in the pure meal of the saints [the Qumran community], for they shall not be cleansed unless they turn from evil-doing; for all who transgress his word are unclean."

Given the general Mediterranean cultural delight in deception and lying, prophets and reformers affirmed that God is not pleased with or duped by pretense or sham. A person who resolved to turn or return to God had better be sincere and honest in every dimension of the ritual. Such a person had better do what the ritual washing symbolizes.

How does a modern American believer hear the Baptizer's message? Living in a prosperous and powerful nation "under God," where God's blessings seem everywhere evident, what does an American believer have to convert "from"? And what does this believer have to turn "to"? These questions are not easy to answer, but this week of Advent is an opportune time to think about them. We will hear the Baptizer's suggestions next week.

Third Sunday of Advent
Luke 3:10-18

How does a person confirm personal repentance? By behaving in an observably different way. The Baptizer offers concrete examples for different categories of people.

FAMILY

In the Middle East it is a common cultural belief that if someone gains more of something, someone else automatically has less. If someone has two coats, the assumption is that someone else has none. And in this culture the desire to have more than one needs is greed, pure and simple. It is shameful.

However, one would not be obliged to go outside the extended family to give away the second coat. One could satisfy the cultural obligation by giving it to another family member. That, after all, is who the Old Testament understands as one's "neighbor" (see Deut 15:2).

This level of sharing is even more apparent in the case of sharing food (Luke 3:10), since peasants live at subsistence levels and never have surplus to distribute beyond the family. It will be a while in this Gospel before Jesus manages to persuade hungry folk to a wider degree of sharing (Luke 9:10-17). Their vision was quite limited to the extended family circle, but even here greed and selfishness often intervened (Luke 12:13-15). For this reason the Baptizer urges that family relationships be placed in a more wholesome balance.

TOLL COLLECTORS

The American system of taxes has little if anything in common with the ancient Roman system. The Greek word that Luke uses here identifies these people as toll collectors. It was their job to collect tolls on goods entering, leaving, or being transported across a district as well as on goods passing crossover points like bridges, gates, or landings.

These toll collectors to whom the Baptizer refers here (and in 5:27, 29, 30; 7:29, 34; 15:1; 18:10, 11, 13) worked for a person like Zacchaeus (Luke 19:2), a "chief" toll collector. In the Roman Empire a chief toll collector was usually a native who bid for the right to collect tolls but had to pay the assessment to Rome immediately upon winning the bid. It was then his task to recoup this sum and make a profit if possible.

Employees of the chief toll collector were often homeless folk with no roots, thus totally incapable of finding other work. The evidence indicates that any cheating or extortion on their part would benefit their employer rather than their personal pockets. Still, many of these employees were fair and honest. And very few of the chief tax collectors were "rich" like Zacchaeus. The entire system was risky, open to abuse, and far from profitable.

So the Baptizer addresses mainly the employees of the chief toll collectors and urges them to be satisfied with "the amount prescribed for you" (Luke 3:13), that is, their commission. This is culturally sound common sense. He says nothing about reforming this oppressive system.

SOLDIERS

There were no Roman legions stationed in Palestine at this time, and Palestinian Judeans were exempt from service in Roman armies since the time of Julius Caesar. These soldiers, therefore, are best understood as Judean men enlisted in the service of Herod Antipas. The soldiers were despised because they worked for Rome's puppet king and strove to enforce the will of Rome, the occupying power. That they are moved to "conversion" is as remarkable as the toll collectors' desire for a better life.

Literally, the Baptizer says "shake no one down or threaten to report to authorities." In other words, don't practice extortion or blackmail. Be content with your pay, or rations and provisions. This is nothing more than the ideal of military conduct proposed by Caesar Augustus.

In the three samples of John's preaching presented by Luke, the evangelist seems unable or unwilling to propose reform of unjust tax systems or to encourage conscientious objection. Indeed, true to Luke's intention of convincing Gentiles that Christians are not a threat to Roman civilization, he portrays the military in a positive light (see also 7:1-10; 23:47).

The impact of John's preaching is nonetheless important: "The people were piqued with curiosity." Could John be the Messiah? No, John distinguishes himself very carefully from "the one who is to come."

What is an American believer to make of the Baptizer's exhortations? Greed, selfishness, and abuse of power and position are still with us. Who among us will be the modern voice crying in the wilderness? Who will call us to conversion and invite us to live fully the good news?

Fourth Sunday of Advent
Luke 1:39-45

Today's simple gospel story is familiar to Christians as "the visitation." Artists have interpreted it on canvas, but how do modern American readers hear and interpret it? Of course, no one imagines Mary getting into the pickup and traveling over the Interstate to do lunch with Elizabeth. But what do they imagine? Here is the scenario that Mediterranean culture suggests.

WOMEN AND TRAVEL

Women in the ancient Middle East could never do anything alone. They either had to be always in a cluster of women and children or under the watchful eye of their father, brother, husband, or some other responsible male relative. A woman, but especially a fourteen-year-old unmarried girl like Mary, who goes anywhere alone is open to charges of shameful intentions and conduct. If no one other than Joseph knew she was pregnant at this time, such a solo journey would leave no doubt in anyone's mind about her pregnancy afterward.

The trip from Nazareth in Galilee where Mary lived to a village in Judea where Elizabeth lived would take four days. (Later Christian tradition identified Ain Karem, eight kilometers west of Jerusalem, as the place.) Since travel alone was not safe, people commonly joined a caravan. This is a possibility for Mary, but Luke does not mention it.

Is there a plausible cultural explanation for Mary's solo journey? We'll consider that possibility next.

LEAPING CHILDREN

It is often difficult for sophisticated contemporary believers to suspend their scientific knowledge in order to understand simpler human explanations. Only in the last 100 to 150 years have we learned the facts of reproduction and child-bearing. Our ancestors in the Faith held a much simpler view of life.

The ancients believed that the male deposited a miniature, fully formed human being in the female. The male provided a "seed"; the woman was the "field." In this worldview, "conception" difficulties are entirely the fault of the field and not of the seed.

Pregnant women have always experienced movement of the child in the womb. Rebekah felt movement and perhaps even suspected that she was bearing twins (Genesis 25). That movement was interpreted as a struggle between the children, symbolizing the future struggle of the two nations they represented (Gen 25:22-23).

Elizabeth interprets the movement of her child in her womb as a "leap prompted by joy" at hearing Mary's greeting. When Elizabeth tells this to her kinswoman, Mary may well have been confirmed in another growing conviction about her own child. Just as the angel announced, her yet unborn child is holy (Luke 1:35). This holiness is a quality that can ward off or protect against evil.

In modern technical jargon, the unborn child's holiness is an "apotropaic" power, that is, a force stronger than evil and evil spirits. Mary could easily conclude that it is safe for her to travel alone because she would be protected by her child's special power, just as Tobit (5:4ff.) was protected by the disguised angel Raphael on his journey abroad. Contemporary cultural descendants of our ancestors in the Faith in the Middle East rely heavily on talismans and similar charms (often blue in color) to protect them from evil.

LUKE'S INTERPRETATION

In 1964 the Pontifical Biblical Commission noted that the evangelists "selected certain things out of the many which had been handed on; some they synthesized; and some they explained with an eye to the situation of the churches." This passage in Luke is considered something he developed as a literary artist and theologian. It is not from the memoirs of Mary. Mary would be an unfeeling kinswoman to leave Elizabeth (as she does in v. 56) at the moment of her greatest need, childbirth!

Luke is surely aware of the cultural inconsistencies and improbabilities of his story. So are his original readers. But they easily recognize Luke's intent. He wanted to explain a dimension of the origins of John the Baptizer and Jesus for his readers. Thus he brings together the two mothers-to-be to show how both recognize and praise the God who is actively involved in their humdrum lives.

Americans are notorious for their weak knowledge of history, especially of anything that happened prior to their date of birth. So it is strange indeed when American believers try to pursue the literal facticity of biblical stories such as this, which serve an entirely different purpose. We can only admire the magnificent talent and inspiration of Luke the evangelist, who has made his point emphatically if imaginatively graphic. God does indeed work in strange and mysterious ways.

Holy Family
Luke 2:41-52

In Mediterranean agrarian societies boys and girls are brought up together, until the age of puberty, by all the women (mother, aunts, sisters, etc.).

MOTHERS AND SONS

No wonder that the strongest emotional bond in the Mediterranean family is between mother and (oldest) son. This bond gives the mother enormous power over the son's life even into adulthood. Recall Rebekah's meddling in the lives of her adult sons, Jacob and Esau (Genesis 25).

Another consequence is that boys who approach the age of puberty are invariably spoiled. Because boys are highly valued in this culture, all the women pamper and pleasure them. For instance, a boy is breast-fed twice as long as a girl, even long after he is able to speak (see 2 Macc 7:27). When he asks for food, he is immediately fed. He concludes that his every word to women is like law.

A third consequence of raising boys and girls together to the nearly total exclusion of the father and other men during the nurturing process is that boys enter puberty with an ambiguous identity. Having had no male role-model, they do not know how to be a man.

At puberty the boy is unceremoniously shoved out of the comfort of the women's world into the harsh and hierarchical men's world. Here all the men teach the adolescent his proper place and behavior. Often this is accomplished by physical punishment or beatings, which he is taught must be suffered in silence without retaliation (see Prov 13:24; 19:18; 22:15; 23:13-14; 29:15, 17; Sir 30:1-12). He naturally concludes such stoic suffering is one way of demonstrating manliness (Isa 42:2; 50:6; 53:3, 7; 2 Maccabees 6–7).

Today's gospel is best viewed against this cultural backdrop. Why was Jesus not missed by his parents until after a day's journey in the homeward direction? The adolescent Jesus was probably still in the process of transition to adulthood. In the caravans people traveled according to the gender divisions that permeate this society: men and boys past the age of puberty traveled together; women and young children (boys and girls) traveled together.

Joseph probably sighed when he discovered that Jesus was absent from the company of men. He may have concluded that Jesus was still struggling with his transition from women's company and ran back to its comfort. In contrast, Mary may have proudly if wistfully believed that Jesus at last was with the men, as would be appropriate for a lad of his age. Only after a day's journey, when Jesus could not be found among male or female relatives and friends, did his family realize he was not in the caravan at all.

JESUS IN THE TEMPLE

When Jesus is finally found, two things emerge in Luke's report. Jesus is meeting with an adult group of men, teachers, in the Temple and giving evidence of intelligent understanding. Luke thus indicates that Jesus has successfully made the transition into the male world.

But the transition has other consequences that are evident in Jesus' dialogue with Mary. The personal irritation reflected in Mary's reproach: "Son, why have you treated us like this?" is perfectly understandable. Jesus is supposed to begin to behave like a responsible, adult male. He obviously did not inform Joseph, Mary, or any friend or relative about his intention. In this group-oriented culture, such independent and individualistic behavior is irresponsible, disrespectful, and shameful.

Jesus' less-than-respectful response ("Did you not know . . . ?") is equally understandable. The plural verb "know" indicates that Jesus reproaches both Mary *and* Joseph. Male maturity in the Mediterranean world entails becoming liberated from the female control that characterizes early childhood. A man wrestles throughout life with the tension between leaving female company behind yet continuing to nurture the strong bond with his mother. Struggling now to trade his mother's tutelage for Joseph's, Jesus is irritated by her reproach.

One possible explanation for Jesus' reproach to Joseph is that he failed to keep a closer eye on and stronger control over him as an adolescent eager to take his rightful place in his appropriate, controlling, all-male group. Did Joseph not care enough about him?

Raising children has never been easy in any culture. Sometimes the only thing that parents can do is to ponder the mystery and hope the child will (continue to) grow in wisdom, maturity, and favor among human beings and God.

Epiphany
Matthew 2:1-12

THE DISCOVERY OF CHILDHOOD

Childhood is a relatively recent discovery, hardly more than two hundred years old. Of course there have always been children and a stage of growth known as childhood. Different cultures, however, have interpreted this period of life very differently.

In the West in general and in the United States in particular, childhood forms a rather lengthy time with distinctive stages. Indeed, some stages of childhood constitute a veritable subculture.

In contrast, the ancient Mediterranean world focused on adults. Childhood was a very brief period of life during which a "miniature adult" was expected to develop as quickly as possible into a full-grown, responsible adult. Its literature speaks of sons and daughters rather than children, and it describes how these should grow to be honorable men and women.

Famous adults were provided with stereotypical "biographies." A stock of virtues would be attributed to that person and applauded. An equally stereotypical childhood would be created in which the future achievements of the adult would already be prefigured from the earliest days. From Roman antiquity, Suetonius' *Lives of the Caesars* offers a good example.

A STORY FROM JESUS' CHILDHOOD

Scholars do not consider Matthew's report about the Magi who come to visit Jesus at his birth as historical fact. It is rather a rich, traditional reflection upon Scripture, perhaps the story of Balaam in Numbers 22–24, intended to demonstrate that Gentile believers are an integral part of God's plan from the very beginning!

In Matthew's story line, representatives from the nations to whom the risen Jesus sends his disciples (Matt 28:19) are already present at the beginning of Jesus' life (Matt 2:1-12).

CREATIVE INTERPRETATION OF SCRIPTURE

Just as our ancestors in the Faith frequently reflected upon and interpreted their Scriptures creatively to help them understand and explain Jesus, so too did their Christian descendants throughout the ages continue that creative reflection upon Matthew's story of the Magi's visit to the newborn Jesus.

In this latter process, the number of visitors (never mentioned by Matthew) varied from two (see the art in the Roman catacombs of Sts. Peter and Marcellinus) to twelve (in some medieval Eastern lists). Matthew's mention of three gifts prompted the conclusion that there were three visitors. Early on (end of the second century), these Magi, or astrologers/astronomers (these disciplines were not yet distinct), were elevated to royalty. A tradition dating from about A.D. 700 describes one of the visitors as "black-skinned and heavily bearded" and named Balthasar.

LANGUAGE

Other elements of Matthew's story developed through a gradual change in understanding ancient languages. In today's liturgy Matthew's story of the Magi is linked with a reading from Isaiah, who says in part: "A multitude of camels shall cover you, the young camels of Midian and Ephah; all those from Sheba shall come. They shall bring gold and frankincense" (60:6).

Contemporary archaeologists identify the biblical Sheba (Hebrew spelling) with Seba or Saba (South Arabic spelling), a portion of southwest Arabia that today is known as Yemen. This region was well irrigated and fertile but also blessed with a major caravan route traversing it and trafficking in frankincense and myrrh. In addition, Sabean ships ranged to Africa and India and returned with a variety of goods, including other spices in addition to frankincense and myrrh.

Language specialists note that the Hebrew word for gold, *zahab*, reflects an earlier Hebrew word, *dahab*. But in South Arabic there is a word from this same root *(dhb)* that refers to spices or gums that produce fragrant odors when burned.

Thus the "gold and frankincense" from Saba mentioned by Isaiah were very likely spices, "gold" being a kind of incense. At some point in time the Hebrew understanding of "gold" as a metal replaced the understanding of "gold" as a kind of incense in this passage, and a "new" interpretation arose. Indications of how this shift in understanding occurred appear in references to the "gold" that was used on the "golden altar" (Heb 9:4; Rev 8:3; 9:13; see Luke 1:11).

Such confusion over the meaning of words was common in antiquity and even more common today in the United States, where the knowledge of foreign languages is not a cultural strength. This factor keeps the strange cultural world of Jesus a puzzle to us. Consider how easily it might be remedied.

Baptism of the Lord
Luke 3:15-16, 21-22

Like many who heard John the Baptist's preaching (Luke 3:1-14), Jesus the artisan was moved to submit to his baptism. Scholars believe that with this baptism Jesus also became a disciple of John's, and until John was imprisoned and put to death, Jesus himself administered John's baptism to others (see John 3:22; 4:2).

THE BAPTISM OF JESUS

In the reports by Matthew, Mark, and Luke of Jesus' baptism, the testimony of the voice from heaven is very important. Jesus is identified as "my Son, the beloved, with whom I am well pleased" (Luke 3:22).

The ancient Mediterranean world believed that the male deposited a fully formed miniature adult (a seed) into the female (viewed simply as a field for the seed). Not yet having achieved the contemporary understanding of human reproduction and lacking the sophisticated paternity tests of our modern era (see Num 5:11-31 for their test), these people were totally unable to prove paternity at the biological level.

For this reason, the public and social acknowledgment of paternity by the male was of critical importance. This act not only gave the child legitimacy and appropriate social standing in the community but also publicly obliged the father to accept responsibility for the child. In Luke's version of Jesus' baptism, the voice from heaven acknowledges Jesus as "my Son, my beloved, with whom I am well pleased."

What kind of human experience was this in which Jesus hears a voice from heaven speaking to him? Scholars note that it is an experience in an altered state of consciousness or an experience of alternate reality. On average, 90 percent of the world's cultures regularly have such experiences and find them useful and meaningful in their cultural context. Only the industrialized West has managed to block this pan-human potential. Even scholars who would insist that the baptism of Jesus is an interpretation from the evangelist's hand must admit that the evangelist built wisely on the culture and made the point with very persuasive cultural plausibility. The transfiguration of Jesus and the appearances of the risen Jesus also belong to this category of human experience.

THE GENEALOGY

Genealogies in the ancient world served many different purposes and were frequently rewritten to suit the purpose. Matthew's genealogy of Jesus opens the Gospel and affirms his identity as a son of David and son of Abraham (Matt 1:1-17). Luke's genealogy is located immediately after the voice from heaven claims Jesus as beloved and pleasing Son (Luke 3:23-38). Like an echo of the voice from heaven, every entry in this genealogy repeats the phrase "son of" as if to emphasize the divine testimony about Jesus. In the final phrases Jesus is identified as son of Adam, son of God. This is exactly what the voice said!

HONOR AND GENEALOGIES

Another function of a genealogy is to document and validate one's social status, one's honor rating. Genealogies in antiquity were regularly rewritten to make this point, as the two different genealogies reported by Luke and Matthew demonstrate. No matter what specific nuance each evangelist intended to make, both were definitely concerned with presenting Jesus as an honorable person.

This was especially important in Jesus' case, given the unusual circumstances of his conception. The genealogies leave no doubt about Jesus' honorable standing in society, no matter what his origins. From this perspective genealogies are also maps that guide social interaction. The people at Nazareth who asked only, "Is this not Joseph's son?" (Luke 4:22) either forgot or did not know the whole of Jesus' status as mapped out in the genealogy.

HONOR AND EVIL SPIRITS

The honor ascribed to Jesus publicly at his baptism and emphasized in Luke's genealogy has yet another consequence in the gospel story line. In each of the synoptic Gospels (Matthew, Mark, and Luke), the baptism of Jesus is followed by the temptation in the desert. In the Mediterranean world every claim to honor invites a challenge. Individuals are eager to test the honorable person to see if they might cause the honorable person to falter, to be shamed.

When the voice from heaven ascribes to Jesus an exceptional honor rating, everyone in the culture would expect that the rating would be challenged, especially by one or another spirit that crowds the air surrounding human beings. Jesus does not falter. Instead, he lives up to his honorable status. More, by resisting the temptations and vanquishing his challenger, Jesus' honor rating grows. This victory adds achieved honor to the honor that was ascribed to him by the heavenly voice.

Modern-day theological interpretations of baptism as a rite of initiation in the Church often overshadow the basic cultural reality from which the rite developed. A fresh look at the baptism of Jesus in its cultural context helps us appreciate the richness of our tradition.

Second Sunday
in Ordinary Time
John 2:1-12

For a Westerner to properly appreciate the cultural setting of this "first sign of Jesus" in Cana of Galilee, it would be very helpful to view the video film *Wedding in Galilee*. While set in the modern-day occupied West Bank, the film offers many valuable cultural scenarios for understanding Mediterranean weddings.

THE WEDDING AND ITS GUESTS

Weddings in the ancient Mediterranean world were pre-arranged by parents for preselected partners. These commonly were relatives, most often a first cousin if such were available. Recall the women whom the patriarchs married (Gen 24:15; 25:19; 28:1-4).

Most of the invited wedding guests would also be relatives, though nonrelatives could be included too. The fact that Mary and Jesus do not hesitate to interfere in this wedding to remedy the shortage of wine (John 2:4-7) strongly suggests that they were related to the wedding party. It would be very shameful for nonrelative guests to interfere in a wedding.

JESUS AND HIS MOTHER

Jesus' response to Mary is interesting on at least two counts. His customary respectful title of address to the females he encounters throughout the Gospels is indeed "Woman" (see

Matt 15:28; Luke 12:12; John 4:21; 8:10; 20:13). This usage is common in Greek writing as well.

Yet referring to one's mother as "Woman" without further qualification is very unusual in Jesus' cultural world. There is no parallel to this in either Hebrew or Greek literature. While some scholars see a special symbolism in this usage, a very plausible Mediterranean cultural scenario suggests other interpretations.

After birth boys and girls were routinely brought up together exclusively by the women (mother, aunts, sisters). Since boys were highly valued in this culture, they were pampered and spoiled by the women. A strong relationship resembling codependency developed between mothers and sons, especially the eldest son.

When boys entered the male world at the age of puberty, they experienced a rude awakening. This harsh hierarchical world was a contrast to the women's world from which the young man just emerged. To help him develop a masculine identity, other men often punished the young man physically. "He who loves his son will whip him often" and "beat his ribs while he is young or else he will become stubborn and disobey you" are pieces of advice offered to fathers by the sage Jesus Ben Sira (see Sir 30:1, 12).

As he grew into adulthood, a young man tried to weaken those strong emotional ties with females. In a very public society like the Mediterranean world the young man would seek to demonstrate his independence by rejecting the claims of all women upon him, including his mother.

"WHAT TO ME AND TO YOU, WOMAN?"

This phrase, literally translated, is sometimes a response of someone who feels unjustly bothered by another (see Judg 11:12; 2 Chr 35:21; 1 Kgs 17:18; Mark 1:24; 5:7; John 2:4[?]). In other instances the phrase is the answer of someone who refuses to get involved in the affairs of someone else (see 2 Kgs 3:13; Hos 14:8; John 2:4 [?]).

In the light of Mediterranean child-rearing practices described above, one plausible cultural scenario for Jesus' statement to his mother is that Jesus the adult son felt unjustly bothered, perhaps even embarrassed by his mother's comment and implied suggestion that he get involved. His reply would then be an attempt to put distance between himself and his mother to declare further independence.

Another equally plausible cultural scenario for Jesus' statement is that Jesus did not want to interfere in something he believed was none of his/their business. On another occasion, he rejected the honorable invitation to be a mediator between two brothers (Luke 12:13-15) because he judged that the petitioner was motivated by greed rather than by justice denied.

Why does Jesus give in? Perhaps maternal pressure was too difficult to evade. Even in his adulthood, his mother's wish may have been Jesus' command. Or perhaps he was genuinely concerned about preserving family honor at a relative's wedding. The traces of Mediterranean culture embedded and hidden in segments of this story offer us beautiful insights into Jesus the Mediterranean man, who John the evangelist tells us early on in his Gospel "pitched his tent among us" (John 1:14). He's just like us in so many human ways.

Third Sunday
in Ordinary Time
Luke 1:1-4; 4:14-21

In addition to the Gospel of Mark, Luke also used the Greek translation of the Old Testament (the Septuagint) as a source in composing his own Gospel. This is evident from comparing what Jesus is reported to have read from the Isaiah scroll in Luke 4:18-19 with Isaiah 61:1-2 in the Hebrew Bible. The Hebrew and Greek versions differ, and Luke uses the Greek version admirably well to make many points in his Gospel.

LUKE'S GOSPEL

A reader with an eye (or ear) trained to discern patterns in ancient texts notices that the verses of Isaiah read by Luke's Jesus (4:18-19) are arranged in a pattern commonly found in ancient literature:

> A—good news to the poor
> B—release to the captives
> C—SIGHT TO THE BLIND
> B'—freedom to the oppressed
> A'—proclaim year of Lord's favor

This concentric arrangement of ideas leads a reader or listener to realize that the ideas of line A and A' are similar, and the ideas of B and B' are similar. Line C stands out as the focal point of the verses.

In fact, a quick reading of Luke and Acts of the Apostles, his second volume, reveals that one of Jesus' major activities in this Gospel is restoring sight to the blind (7:21) and understanding to the unenlightened. But many people challenge and reject this understanding or insight, whether given by Jesus or by his disciples (see Luke's conclusion to his two-volume work in Acts 28:23-28).

This first scene from Jesus' ministry in Luke's Gospel prepares the reader or listener for what is to come in the remainder of the Gospel. Besides offering new understanding to his audiences (line C), Jesus will free people from bondage (e.g., to demons, lines B and B') and restore meaning to people's lives by healing them (lines A and A'). It is for this total ministry that the Spirit has anointed Jesus. Thus does Luke use the quote from Isaiah to disclose the plan of his Gospel and Acts of the Apostles.

THE SYNAGOGUE SCENARIO

A close examination of this event in the Nazareth synagogue reveals that Luke has combined traditions from a variety of sources to compose a scenario for Jesus' visit to his hometown. The composition is clearly uneven, but it well illustrates the positive and negative reactions that Jesus stirred.

The immediate reaction to Jesus' reading from Isaiah is positive. The hometown crowd in the synagogue is impressed and grants Jesus accolades of honor. "All spoke well of him and were amazed at his speech" (4:22).

Then a doubt begins to arise among them: "Is this not Joseph's son?" Jesus, the carpenter's son, is stepping beyond the bounds of his ascribed honor, that is, the honor he has by birth. In the Mediterranean world, a son takes up the profession of his father and receives the name of his grandfather. If Jesus' father is an artisan, why is he preaching and teaching rather than working with his hands as he ought?

Anticipating a challenge from the townspeople, Jesus delivers an insulting put-down to their as yet unvoiced objection. "Truly I tell you, no prophet is accepted in the prophet's own hometown" (v. 24). The insult is sharpened when Jesus highlights Gentile strangers in verses 25 to 27 as better able to judge the honor of a prophet than those who live in close proximity on a daily basis.

Jesus' insulting put-down is a challenge to the honor of his hometown folk. They must respond forcefully and decisively or they will have been shamed by Jesus. They respond with rage (v. 28) and drive him out of town in order to hurl him off a cliff (v. 29). Jesus, ever the master of the situation, escapes from them unharmed.

He has maintained the honor that is his by birth and achieved yet additional honor by besting his opponents in a spirited exchange.

As presented by the lectionary for today's liturgy, this reading from Luke and its partner from Nehemiah 8 have been stripped of their cultural details in order to highlight the power of the preached word. Restoring details of the cultural context highlights the risky and frightening human dimension of preaching situations. Both preacher and listener face serious risks. Are we up to them?

Fourth Sunday
in Ordinary Time
Luke 4:21-30

In the Mediterranean world of antiquity everyone had a proper place that was established by birth. No one was ever expected to become something better than or to improve on the lot of the parents. This fact is the basic foundation of honor, the public claim to worth, and the public acknowledgment of that worth by others. Each child inherits, carries on, and is expected to safeguard the family's honor.

In today's reading Jesus is perceived by others in his village to be stepping shamefully beyond his family boundaries. The event as Luke reports it reflects the tensions this kind of behavior would raise in any tiny Mediterranean village.

HONOR AND ONE'S FATHER

It is customary in the Mediterranean for a son to carry on his father's trade and his grandfather's name. When the Arab merchant from whom I used to purchase carefully designed and colorfully dyed eggs in Bethlehem died, I was not at all surprised to find his stall and his business still in existence the following year. His young son carries on his father's profession to this day.

The people in Nazareth, Jesus' hometown (1:26; 2:4, 39, 51; Acts 10:38), know him and his family very well. While reducing the townspeople's reaction to Jesus in comparison with Matthew and Mark, Luke nevertheless records their amazement. "Is not this Joseph's son?" Jesus stirs controversy at the very least because he does not seem to be carrying on Joseph's trade. He is doing something different. This is a breach of family honor not readily countenanced in the Mediterranean world.

JESUS THE HEALER

Luke adds to this source of amazement among the towns-people yet another. His addition, though intentional, is clumsy, because at this point in Luke's Gospel Jesus has not yet been to Capernaum, nor has he yet healed anybody.

Instead of practicing his father's trade, Luke's Jesus points to two other activities that he prefers. First, he proclaims for himself and, indeed, practices healing activities. This is the focus of his citation from Isaiah (40:3-5), which Jesus will definitely "fulfill" in his ministry to follow very shortly.

Our contemporary understanding of health and healing is tied rather closely to scientific Western medicine. Thanks to the microscope, we know of the existence, nature, and function of germs. And human beings can do something to keep germs in check, thwart their effects, and even destroy them.

In Jesus' world no one knew about germs or viruses, but they did know that human beings in general had no power over the human experience of illness. When an extraordinary person like Jesus seemed to have power to heal, that is, to restore meaning to people's lives, nearly everyone rejoiced and sought this healer's help. So far so good.

In the Mediterranean world the basic rule is "look after your family first." While in that culture it is a virtue, in our culture it is frowned upon as nepotism. Even in Luke's clumsy story line, Jesus has broken this rule. He has healed the sick in Capernaum but has apparently not healed anyone in his hometown.

JESUS THE PROPHET

Rubbing salt into the wound opened by his insulting behavior (preaching in his hometown, healing elsewhere), Jesus inserts himself into the prophetic line of Elijah and Elishah. Like them, he ministers not to fellow Mediterranean Judeans but rather to Gentiles, non-Judeans, people not of his own kind. To direct his healing activities to such rather than to those of his hometown (very likely blood relatives) is to transgress very seriously against family honor.

It is small wonder that these townspeople became filled with rage and wanted to kill him. Honor in the Mediterranean world is a matter of life and death.

The shocking behavior of the adult Jesus is difficult for Americans to appreciate. In our culture children are expected to do better than their parents. At a rather early age they are expected to go out on their own, get their own apartment, and live as independent human beings. The freedom that parents wish for their children in our culture is captured in the poignant television advertisement in which the elderly insist, "I do not want to be a burden to my children." How very different the family and townsfolk of Jesus, the healing prophet.

Fifth Sunday in Ordinary Time
Luke 5:1-11

THE "CALL" OF DISCIPLES

What would prompt you to abandon your job? higher pay? a better occupation? an improved location? a more congenial employer? all of the above? Jesus' invitation to some fishermen to leave their business and follow after him is best understood in the context of this question.

FISHING

Luke notes that Peter (and of course his brother, Andrew) had a business partnership with another pair of brothers, James and John (Luke 5:10). They owned at least two boats (5:2).

A boat discovered in 1986 close to shore at the Sea of Galilee is 26.5 feet long, 7.5 feet wide, and 4.5 feet high, with a rounded stern and a fine bow. (Carbon tests thus far date this boat to the period 140 B.C. to A.D. 40).

Physical anthropologists estimate that the average Galilean male of the Roman-Byzantine period stood about 5 feet 5 inches tall and weighed an average of 140 pounds. Fifteen such men would weigh just over a ton and could easily fit into this boat.

Jesus stepped into Peter's boat (v. 3). Mark tells us one boat held at least five passengers: James and John, their father Zebedee, and hired men (1:20). There could have been many more.

Fish became a popular commodity in the Greek and Roman period, and it is reasonable to guess that this specific partnership flourished. What prompted them to "leave everything and follow Jesus" (v. 11)? His invitation alone?

PATRONAGE

The act of a man calling followers in Mediterranean culture is readily recognized by every native as a process of a patron gathering clients. In cultures like that where central government was perceived to be weak and ineffective, people banded together for mutual assistance.

For the most part, families stuck close together and helped each other out. But sometimes it became necessary to reach beyond the family and to form "family-like" bonds with others who could lend the help that family members couldn't. One of these others is a "patron," that is, a person with surplus means who distributes that surplus by purely personal whim and choice.

By providing seasoned and experienced fishermen with a bountiful catch after a frustrating night of work, Jesus presents himself very obviously as a patron. A patron is someone who can get for you something you could not obtain by your own abilities, or on better terms than you could arrange for yourself. Jesus gets the better of these fisher folk at their own game! In Luke's story Simon, James, and John clearly perceive Jesus in this role. By falling at the knees of Jesus, Simon Peter uses a specific gesture that recognizes him as superior, as a patron.

THE CLIENTS

Luke notes that Simon and "all who were with him were amazed at the catch of fish they had taken" (v. 9). When they reached shore, "they left everything and followed Jesus" (v. 11). While it is possible that everyone in the boats followed Jesus, we know that Simon, Andrew, James, and John did, but apparently not their respective fathers, Jonah and Zebedee.

The "everything" that they left included much more than boats and nets. It included their social network, which meant other patrons, friends, and neighbors in addition to the relatives (father, mother, wife, in-laws, etc.). Everyone would consider such people crazy, *unless* . . .

Unless they saw in this new patron, Jesus, something they could not get elsewhere. It is not entirely clear what the followers of Jesus, his new clients, saw. Certainly it was more than fish. But they were convinced by this catch of fish, at least in Luke's story, that Jesus was the patron they wanted, the one who could get for them what they really wanted.

THE MODERN WORLD

In mainstream U.S. culture, we take great pride in standing on our own two feet and in not having to rely on anyone else. We applaud those who pull themselves up by their own bootstraps. Our Mediterranean ancestors in the Faith would consider this insane, an invitation to death and extinction. Following Jesus as a client in the Mediterranean world or a disciple in the modern world involves a willingness to be dependent. One gives up apparent security for a perceived greater security. Are Americans up to it? The Galilean fishermen were.

Sixth Sunday
in Ordinary Time
Luke 6:17, 20-26

Mae West observed: "I've been poor, and I've been rich. Believe me, rich is better." What is "blessed" about being poor? Why would Jesus say this? What poor person would believe it? At the very beginning of this reflection, it is important to remember that the word "poor" in biblical culture describes a social reality rather than an economic one.

LIMITED GOODS

In ancient Palestine the peasant population believed that all goods (spiritual as well as material!) exist in a finite quantity. Thus not only grain and livestock but honor, friendship, reputation, love, status, security, power–everything in life is limited and already distributed. If a person loses any of these goods, there simply is no more where that came from.

If this same person suddenly found what was lost, neighbors would be suspicious. They would wonder whether this found item had been stolen from someone else. This was precisely the problem faced by the woman who found her lost coin (Luke 15:8-10). She had no choice but to summon the neighbors and assure them she had not stolen this piece of jewelry but rather found what she had lost.

LIVING WITH LIMITED GOODS

How did this commonly shared cultural belief shape human behavior? It dictated that every person should be satisfied with whatever is rightfully possessed. No one should have a desire to increase possessions. Such a desire could only be interpreted as an expression of greed. The fellow who asked Jesus to force his brother to divide the family inheritance with him was warned: "Beware of all greed!" (Luke 12:15). The Law clearly determined that the elder is to receive double the younger's share (Deut 21:17). Jesus refused to be a partner to greed.

RICH AND POOR

In this cultural context, the labels "rich" and "poor" take on a meaning quite different than in our culture. In antiquity a person became rich because that individual had power to take wealth from those who were weaker and unable to defend themselves. While in the modern Western world wealth itself bestows power, in the ancient Mediterranean world power was the means for acquiring wealth.

By the same token, a poor person in the ancient world was powerless, that is, unable to defend inherited status and wealth. Notice the kinds of people with which the word "poor" is most often associated. As a rule, we read in the Bible about "the poor, the orphans, and the widows." What these categories share in common is a certain deficiency in social relationships and consequent powerlessness.

The orphan has no adults to protect its interests. The widow, even if she possesses millions of denarii but has no son, is regularly described (even to this day in that part of the world) as "a poor widow." Economic considerations enter the picture only incidentally and then only for the wealthy.

The culturally more appropriate translation of "rich" and "poor" in the Bible, therefore, would be "greedy" and "socially unfortunate."

"HOW ESTEEMED, HONORABLE, BLESSED . . ."

What is "blessed" about being socially unfortunate (poor, hungry, and weeping)? A "beatitude" proposes a cultural value, belief, or behavior pattern that is truly honorable. In Mediterranean society, whose core value is honor, everyone wants to know the honorable thing to do. Obviously, being poor, defrauded of one's wealth, persecuted, insulted, and the like are not honorable experiences. Such people would be judged as shamed.

In the Beatitudes, however, Jesus promises a reward from God for those who suffer these shameful experiences. The vast majority of people in the ancient world were poor. This condition was brought about by the greedy wicked folk, not by an economy gone awry, laziness, or bad luck. God is the ultimate arbiter of true honor, and the honor God bestows is unsurpassable. When God honors the socially unfortunate, everyone will know their true status.

Jesus' Beatitudes therefore were primarily words of consolation to people who desperately needed to hear this good news. They also pointed to moral qualities that God-fearing folk should strive to achieve: to know one's place and keep it (poor); to protest social injustice (hungry and weeping, which are ritualized elements of protest activities). People who behave in such honor-deserving ways will indeed be honored by God, which is the only honor that counts. Who can argue with that?

Seventh Sunday in Ordinary Time
Luke 6:27-38

THE GOLDEN RULE

Luke's Jesus commands the disciples: "As you [plural] wish people to treat you, treat them in like manner" (6:31). Matthew's Jesus says: "Whatever you wish people would do for you, do for them yourselves" (7:12). Hillel, a contemporary of Jesus, is reported to have said: "Whatever is hateful to you, do not do to anyone else; that is the whole Law, all else is commentary. Go and learn it" (Babylonian Talmud, Sabbath 31a). There were many variations on this saying in antiquity.

RECIPROCITY

The Mediterranean cultural value behind this "golden rule" is reciprocity. This word describes a variety of give-and-take, or back-and-forth exchanges between individuals or villages, usually along one of three patterns.

General reciprocity is a sharing of goods with no hope of return. This characterizes family relationships. "Is there anyone among you who, if your child asks for bread, will give a stone?" (Matt 7:9). Parents meet the needs of their children but do not keep a strict accounting of the child's debt. It is enough that the child reciprocate with love and gratitude.

Balanced reciprocity characterizes neighborly relations. It is a satisfaction of needs that is mutually beneficial. Luke's Jesus describes–and criticizes–it well. Balanced reciprocity means loving in return those who love you first. Doing good in return to those who do good first. Lending now in the secure hope of being repaid or of being able to borrow from the same person at a future time is another example. Invitations to meals fall in this category, too. Each invitation implies an invitation in return (Luke 14:12-14).

Negative reciprocity characterizes relations with strangers. It is a relationship in which one party hopes to take advantage of the other party, to gain without having to repay anything at all (see Luke 19:22). This pattern of relationship gave rise to the Middle-Eastern custom of hospitality, which is granted mainly by men and exclusively to *strangers.* Such hosts protect strangers from relationships of negative reciprocity in this alien village (see Gen 19:5) and engage instead in a general reciprocity with their guests. They expect no return; indeed, a return of hospitality would be an insult.

THE AUDIENCE OF LUKE'S JESUS

The advice given by Jesus in Luke 6:27-36 is clearly directed to the elite. Only such would have two coats (v. 29), or would be the targets of beggars and thieves (v. 30), or would have surplus wealth to lend (vv. 34–35). Jesus is asking the elite to behave toward strangers just as they would behave toward members of their own household. He is urging the haves to treat have-nots as if they were family. He discourages negative reciprocity, that is, the attempt by the elites to take advantage of those in need. Remember that all this advice is given with the beatitude "How truly honorable and esteemed are the socially unfortunate" still ringing in this elite audience's ears.

STEREOTYPING

The categories "elite" and "socially unfortunate = poor" are products of another common Mediterranean cultural trait that Jesus challenges: stereotyping. This culture is not at all introspective. It routinely judges by external appearances (see 1 Sam 16:7). It is also prone to generalizing and stereotyping people. "All natives of Crete are liars, vicious brutes, and lazy gluttons" (Titus 1:12). "Judeans do not share things in common with Samaritans" (John 4:9). "Can anything good come out of Nazareth?" (John 1:46).

As repulsive as such judgments may sound to modern Western ears, they were very common in the ancient world. People pasted labels on others (sinner, tax collector, woman of the city, carpenter's son, whitewashed sepulcher, etc.) as a means of controlling and restricting their social interactions. Such name calling also attributed a status to them, whether it fit or not. The pity is how easily the stereotype stuck.

Jesus' rejection of such stereotyping efforts also resonates in the echo of the beatitude: "How greatly esteemed [by God, of course], are the poor [socially unfortunate, the stereotyped and rejected]. . . ." God alone reads hearts and knows people's true honor rating.

The familiar Western proverb declares: "Stick and stones may break my bones, but names will never hurt me." We like to believe that we are immune from stereotyping and the exploitation it permits. Our ancestors in the Faith would vigorously disagree. Many Westerners would probably concur. It may be time to revise our proverb.

Eighth Sunday in Ordinary Time
Luke 6:39-45

Non-introspective people who rely on external appearances for judging others develop a skill for creating and projecting appearances. In order to win a positive judgment from others and thereby gain a grant of honor from them, people learn to "put up a front," to "wear a mask."

Devious questioners hoping to trap Jesus compliment him by saying, "Teacher, we know that you show no favor to anyone [literally, you do not *lift up the face*]" (Luke 20:21). While many people were unable to judge by more than what they saw, some, like Jesus, could see through human masks. This was extraordinary.

HYPOCRITES

Imagine the scenario of would-be teachers or leaders who are expert at putting on a mask and offering advice to others regarding moral improvement. In the Middle East this scene is very easy to imagine. It happens all the time. Audiences constantly wonder about the teacher. And the teacher always strives to put on the best front!

Jesus, however, calls these teachers "hypocrites." In classical and Hellenistic Greek this word meant "interpreter," "expounder," "orator," even "stage actor." In this latter case, the Greek word took on the added meaning of "deceiver" and "pretender." In theater this is an award-winning skill. In reality–even in Mediterranean culture–this skill and strategy makes life difficult. Whom can one trust?

In the synoptic Gospels, only Jesus uses the word "hypocrite" to criticize certain people. Here (6:39-42) he identifies misguided teachers and leaders as such. Later in this Gospel he calls the crowd "hypocrites," who know how to "interpret the appearance [literally, face!] of the earth and sky, but not how to interpret the present time" (Luke 12:56). In the next chapter, he again scolds the crowds who object to his healing a woman on the Sabbath: "Hypocrites! Don't you rescue your ox or donkey on the sabbath when necessary? Why should I not rescue this woman?" (13:15). In each instance, Jesus sees through the facades each group constructs.

In the Sermon on the Plain, Jesus exhorts his listeners to candid self-examination and authentic efforts to improve self before attempting to help others improve themselves. Short of this effort, such teachers and leaders are blind, unreliable, and untrustworthy. They are deceivers, actors, hypocrites!

BEARING GOOD FRUIT

Another way of identifying hypocrites in the ancient world was to notice inconsistency in behavior. Our ancestors in the Faith believed that human beings should behave consistently, even though many of them did not.

How was consistency determined? The human body could be divided into three distinct yet interpenetrating *symbolic* zones: eyes-heart (the eyes for gathering the information that the heart needs for making judgments); mouth-ears (the organs that collect and share self-expressive speech); and hands-feet (the body parts that act upon or implement what one has learned or knows).

Eyes-heart. Jesus spoke of teachers and guides with flawed vision (6:39-42). He noted the heart's potential for producing both good and evil. He urged that teachers strive to develop proper vision and insight and a good heart.

Mouth-ears. For Jesus, it is clearly imperative that a person cultivate a good heart that will produce good fruit, "for it is out of the abundance of the heart that the mouth speaks" (v. 45), words that others will hear, remember, and act upon.

Hands-feet. But speaking alone is not enough. "Why do you call me, 'Lord, Lord' and *do not do* what I tell you?" (v. 46). It is imperative to act upon what one knows, to live according to what one has learned.

This is how the human person acts consistently, with all the symbolic body parts in sync: heart-eyes, mouth-ears, hands-feet. In other words, it is important that one's emotion-fused thoughts (heart-eyes), self-expressive speech (mouth-ears), and purposeful activity (hands-feet) be perfectly coordinated. Anything else is stage-acting.

If our ancestors in the Faith could spy on us as we are spying on them, they would consider us as strange as we consider them. But on this we would agree. Human beings owe each other—and God—honesty and integrity in every dimension of life.

Ninth Sunday in Ordinary Time
Luke 7:1-10

The key to understanding this story and Jesus' role as a first-century healer is the Mediterranean institution known as "patronage." In the Mediterranean world of antiquity, central government was perceived by the citizens to be ineffectual in meeting their needs. In all such instances, citizens must look after their own needs.

Mediterranean peasants look after their own needs in two ways. One, the way of mutual obligation: "I do you a favor. Now you owe me a favor. When you return the favor, I owe you another," in a never-ending process. Two, the way of recourse to a patron, that is, someone who can obtain for the client whatever the client could not obtain by personal effort, or on better terms than could be obtained by personal effort. When one's social equals cannot come through, one has recourse to a "social superior," that is, a patron.

THE CENTURION

This high-ranking officer represents Rome to the local community, and he brokers favors and resources from Rome to the local citizenry. The fact that he has provided funds for the construction of a synagogue qualifies him as a patron. The delegation to Jesus is correct in saying that "he loves our nation." A patron by definition freely chooses his clients and freely elects to treat them "as if they were family, personally related." This is what family love in the Mediterranean world entails.

THE JUDEAN ELDERS

In this story the Judean elders are connected with the synagogue, perhaps as the "board of elders" that administered the community's affairs. As such they are "clients" of the centurion. They are in his debt for building the synagogue.

It is easy to understand that one way of honoring their patron, the centurion, is to become "middle-men" or "go-betweens" with Jesus on behalf of the centurion. The elders' role is simply that of messengers: they bring the centurion's request to Jesus and hope, indeed will pressure Jesus, for a favorable response.

In Jesus' presence, these elders fulfill another common obligation of a client: they sing the praises of their patron to Jesus. Since this meeting is quite public, everyone in earshot hears about the good qualities of the centurion who loves these Judean people and treats them "as if they were family."

THE CENTURION AND JESUS

The centurion desires a healing intervention from Jesus on behalf of his sick slave. By sending a second delegation, "friends," to Jesus with a special message "don't bother to come under my roof," the centurion masterfully employs additional key elements in the culture to spell out his relationship to Jesus.

The centurion sees Jesus as a social superior. After all, the centurion is not a native; he is a resident alien capable of brokering imperial privilege and commanding a small entourage. But Jesus, the healing-prophet, is a native of this country. As a prophet and healer in Israel, he a broker between the God of Israel and God's sick people.

Outsiders, like the centurion, see Jesus as a powerful patron. It would be awkward for one powerful patron to interact with another powerful patron. The risk of shame would be high, because one of these would be made to look like the other one's client. The centurion is well aware and does not intend to project this challenge, hence he relies on go-betweens like the Judean elders (his clients) and his personal friends (who by definition are obligated to him) to intercede for him with Jesus.

In particular, the centurion recognizes something that the Israelites refuse to see: Jesus' authority or power to heal (see Luke 20:2). Jesus' response to the centurion's friends spells it out explicitly: "Truly, not even in Israel have I found faith or loyalty like this!" The centurion's slave is effectively healed.

Contemporary believers may find this view of life amusing. In the West we know that money speaks. A shopping center in Baltimore, Maryland, adopted the slogan: "Money can buy happiness if you know where to shop." Then, so the consumer won't have to think about the true nature of happiness, it lists all the stores in the shopping center. In the Western view, forget family, friends, patrons, or the cultivation of personal relationships. In matters of human well-being, the West offers the best health care that money can buy. One need not be friends with the healer; one simply must be able to afford the healer. Pity the Western person with friends but without money. What a contrast with the world of Jesus!

Tenth Sunday in Ordinary Time
Luke 7:11-17

Which "dead" person in this story has been restored to life?

The central character in this healing story is much more likely the widowed mother rather than the deceased son. Insights from Mediterranean culture help place the story in proper focus.

WOMEN IN THE MEDITERRANEAN WORLD

As the biblical books of Proverbs and Sirach amply illustrate, women in the Mediterranean world must always be under the care of a key man in their lives: father, brother, husband, or son. While women have enormous power in the Mediterranean world, they wield it differently and in different spheres than do men.

A wayward single daughter risks bringing shame upon the entire family if she should be taken advantage of. An older unmarried daughter has failed to strengthen the family through marriage (Sir 42:9-10). Marriages in the Mediterranean world united families and always were contracted with a view to family advantage.

A divorced woman brings shame because she must return to her father and family of origin. The family strengthened by the advantageous union is now returned to its former, weaker social position. Moreover, the father must return the bride-price. And no one is likely to marry the divorcée.

The woman in today's story is particularly vulnerable. She is a widow, which means she has already lost the primary male obliged to look after her. Now she has lost her only son, her only source of support and her last connection to her husband's family. We do not know that this was her only child. She may have daughters, but in this world daughters are of little help. If single, they are as vulnerable as the widow. If married, they have already transferred to their husband's family.

MOTHERS AND SONS

In the Mediterranean world of antiquity as well as the present, the closest emotional bond is between mother and oldest son. The weakest emotional bond is between husband and wife. (Recall that the traditional Mediterranean marriage is usually arranged and the partners are customarily cousins, typically first degree.)

Because a woman has no identity in her husband's family until she bears a son, the male child is a source of great joy and security for a mother. Young boys are brought up together with the young girls exclusively by the women in the family until the age of puberty. During this period mothers and the other women pamper the boys, pleasure them, and make them very dependent even into adulthood.

THE WIDOW OF NAIN

Of course the son is dead. But so too is his mother. Without any significant male in her life to take care of her, this woman is as good as dead in her society. Though she still possesses physical life, it is bereft of meaning.

Jesus is moved to compassion by the sight of this widow following her only son's bier. It is a compassion he has earlier enjoined on his followers: "Be compassionate as your heavenly father is compassionate" (Luke 6:36). This compassion leads to action. He raises the boy and presents him to his mother.

If healing is understood in antiquity as the restoration of meaning to life, then whose life has had great meaning restored to it in this story? Contemporary Western individuals who have had a "near-death" experience and then were "resuscitated" or "restored to life" frequently recount their disappointment in returning to "this world." While we cannot validly apply these experiences to antiquity, it would seem that the young man restored to life was restored to a comfortably secure male existence in Mediterranean culture.

The widowed mother, on the other hand, who lost her son, lost everything of value in her world. Even her life lost meaning. To have her son restored by Jesus is to have been given a new lease on meaningful life in that world.

Modern Western believers are heavily influenced by scientific Western perspectives and ponder what it might mean "scientifically" for a young man to be "restored to life." For all the good that science has bestowed upon us, it has often robbed us of the ability to see dimensions of life such as those presented in this gospel story.

Which "dead" person has been restored to life in this story? What do you think?

First Sunday of Lent
Luke 4:1-13

The Mediterranean world lives by a deeply rooted belief in spirits who exist in numbers too huge to count and whose major pastime is interfering capriciously in daily human life. Individual Mediterranean cultures, like the Italian or Spanish, rely upon a broad range of amulets, formulas, or other symbols to ward off attacks from spirits.

In this world blue is a favorite color believed to be an especially powerful protection against spirits. People there paint the window frames and doorjambs blue or wear blue ribbons or clothes precisely for this reason. Others wear specific medals, charms, amulets, which are guaranteed to impede attacks.

Now when the voice from heaven identified Jesus at his baptism as "my Son, the Beloved; with you I am *well pleased*" (Luke 3:22), all the spirits heard this compliment (See Baptism of the Lord, above). Every Mediterranean native knows what must and will happen next in Jesus' life. Spirits will test him to determine whether the compliment is indeed true, and just in case it might be true, the spirits will try to make Jesus do something *displeasing* to God.

It is no surprise, then, that the very next scene in Jesus' life that Luke presents is "the temptation." Jesus was full of the Holy Spirit. He was led by a good spirit into the wilderness, the normal habitat of spirits, where he did battle with an evil spirit, the devil.

49

What is totally surprising in Luke's narrative is that Jesus is not reported to be wearing blue garments or using an amulet or even special formulas for protection. Rather, he engages in direct one-on-one dialogue with this evil spirit in a Scripture-quoting contest.

Three times Jesus is tempted to do something that would make him a displeasing son. Three times Jesus replies with a quote from Scripture (Deut 8:3; 6:13; 6:16) to vanquish the temptation. The devil also quotes Scripture to Jesus (Ps 91:11-12, the responsorial psalm for this Sunday) but still does not succeed in tripping him up. Jesus wins the contest, and the devil leaves him "until an opportune time" (see Luke 22:3).

The temptation story is based upon and carefully crafted after the pattern of Israel's temptations in the desert during its Exodus from Egypt. Luke arranged the temptations differently from Matthew in order to end with the Jerusalem Temple as the final temptation. Jerusalem and the Temple is a key motif for Luke, as the mountain is for Matthew.

Clearly, the story of Jesus' victory over the devil is not intended by Luke as a model for baptized Christians who also have to battle against evil spirits. No Christian possesses the powers that Jesus is here tempted to misuse.

Luke's purpose in this temptation story is to present Jesus precisely as the kind of person John the Baptist predicted: the "more powerful one" (Luke 3:16). Indeed, later in this Gospel Jesus will describe himself and his activity with the same phrase: only a "more powerful one" or "one stronger" than the devil can cast out demons (Luke 11:22).

Those among Luke's first readers who asked, "why should I believe in Jesus?" are given culturally appropriate answers. Jesus displays an extraordinary degree of control over life and nature. He possesses an ability to safeguard and maintain his honor and avoid shame. Until his arrest, trial, and death, no one—human or spirit—succeeds in shaming him, tripping him up, or causing him to fall from his stated position and goals. He is indeed a "more powerful one."

Americans in general do not believe that spirits cause them any problems. This cultural conviction is what made the comedian Flip Wilson's character, Geraldine, so amusing as often as she resorted to her favorite excuse: "The devil made me do it!"

But Americans do understand power. They especially understand and resent abuse of power by those who should wield it for the benefit of others. Scholars point out that in the Gospels Jesus wields no power at all except in regard to spirits and demons. Viewed from this perspective, the story of Jesus' refusal to abuse the power he had offers Americans something very relevant to ponder.

Second Sunday of Lent
Luke 9:28-36

In her recent study of the transfiguration of Jesus, Chicago biblical scholar and Dominican Sister Barbara Reid concluded that Luke's account probably contains the earliest form of the story. Two men appeared in glory and spoke of Jesus' "exodus," which he was to fulfill in Jerusalem. Peter and those with him saw Jesus' glory and the two men standing with him. The two men are most likely angels presenting an instructive message about forthcoming events for earthbound listeners. Influenced by Mark, the Lucan redactor equated these angels with Moses and Elijah and added other information from Mark.

Like many historical-critical biblical scholars, Reid considers the evidence of this text as too fragmentary to provide scientifically certain results about what that experience really might have been. Such skepticism, however, is unwarranted. It is based upon the unexamined and unquestioned Western cultural biases that so permeate science as to be almost indistinguishable from it.

Scientific cultural analyses of 488 societies from all the world's cultures have discovered that 90 percent of these societies routinely and normally experience alternate realities in waking visions or trances. The phrase that describes such a human experience is "altered state of consciousness."

Even scientifically minded Americans are familiar with some of these experiences. A favorite piece of music, a cherished painting, or even a glass of wine can produce changes in consciousness. Generally speaking, however, Americans distrust whatever they cannot control. Experiences of alternate reality are spontaneous, *if* one allows them to happen. But since the development of science in the seventeenth century, Westerners have successfully blocked access to these experiences and tend to distrust or discredit those who have them.

In the ancient Mediterranean world, experiences of alternate reality in vision and trance were common. Devotees of the healing god, Asclepius, routinely learned about their illness and appropriate therapy for it from this god in a "sacred" dream. Prophets like Isaiah (6:1-13), Jeremiah (1:11-19), and Ezekiel (1:4-28) described their experiences of God in alternate reality. The entire book of Revelation is a report of what the author, John, experienced in an altered state of consciousness that could be called "ecstacy" or "trance" (the literal Greek is "in spirit" in Rev 1:10; 4:2; 17:3; 21:10).

In Luke's Gospel, the baptism of Jesus (3:21-22) could be viewed as an experience of alternate reality in which one could see the heavens opened and the Holy Spirit in the form of a dove, and hear a voice from heaven speaking intelligibly. The Lucan temptation story, created as it is by tradition (cf. Mark 1:12-13), can also be interpreted as an experience of alternate reality in an altered state of consciousness.

The transfiguration story makes good, culturally plausible sense as another such experience. It is similar to an ancient report by a translator of a book of healings by Asclepius. He took ill and went with his mother to the temple for healing. In a waking vision, she saw the god come to him, and when she woke him to relate what she saw, before she could say anything he informed her that he saw the same in his own dream.

Jesus and his select circle of disciples share an experience of alternate reality. The text does not tell us what Jesus saw or heard, only that his face gave external indication of his experience. The text reports what Peter, James, and John saw and heard. The scene concludes with an assurance from heaven: "This is my Son, my chosen, listen to him."

A common function of experiences of alternate reality is to provide enlightenment about some puzzle, or guidance regarding a proper course of action to take. In Luke's story line, Jesus' teaching and healing activities gain for him friends (4:38-39; 8:40) and enemies (5:21; 6:46; 7:31, 39; 8:43). His fellow villagers (4:29) and others (6:11) wanted to kill him.

It would take an experience like the transfiguration to set the minds of Jesus and his chosen followers at ease. In spite of ominous signs, God was pleased with Jesus and encouraged the trio to heed what he says. Even if a scholar insisted in denying that this is what "really" happened, the scenario makes very plausible Mediterranean sense. One can only admire an evangelist who created the scene if it did not happen in actual fact.

The Western infatuation with science has brought in its wake blessings and curses. No one can deny the many benefits that science produces. The challenge is not to lose precious human gifts like the capacity for mystical experiences and other experiences of alternate reality that hold an honored place in Christian tradition and piety.

Third Sunday of Lent
Luke 13:1-9

This pair of stories (1-5 and 6-9) highlights once more the centrality of politics and political concerns in the ministry of Jesus.

In the highly charged atmosphere of Roman-occupied first-century Palestine, atrocity storytellers report a rumor (unattested anywhere in contemporary literature) to Jesus about Pilate's murder of worshipers offering sacrifice. This lie is a trap.

If Jesus follows the advice of Amos 5:13 and keeps silent, he will be accused of insensitivity, disloyalty, perhaps even treason. What patriot dares question revolution and guerilla warfare? If Jesus criticizes Pilate, he will surely be reported to Roman authorities and punished by them.

Too often those who suffer political oppression and their defenders assume that political suffering is the only kind that counts. They become indifferent to other suffering, especially if it comes from a nonpolitical source.

This is why Jesus' response moves the discussion from political rumor to personal sin and suffering, and he concludes with an exhortation that *all* must repent! Jesus turns attention from the hated oppressor (Pilate/Rome) and focuses it instead on the complainers. *They* should forget Pilate and worry about their own relationship to God. One can only wonder why the questioners did not turn on Jesus and kill him on the spot at this moment, as they had tried in a similar confrontation in the Nazareth synagogue (Luke 4:29).

If you want your protest movement to succeed, remember that there is both good and evil among the protesters just as there is good and evil among the oppressors.

THE BARREN FIG TREE

While the preceding discussion concerned the people, this one unmistakably concerns the leaders (= fig tree) who are stealing life from the people (= the vineyard; see Isa 5:7). Later in this Gospel (Luke 20:19) the leadership (scribes and chief priests) clearly understands that vineyard parables are directed to them and told about them. Thus this present parable unmistakably states that current leadership within the nation is fruitless and should be rooted out.

The details of this parable reflect its Mediterranean cultural context perfectly. The vineyard owner obviously lives in the city and rents his vineyard to a tenant farmer who does the digging, the planting, etc. He "had the tree planted."

The Palestinian fig tree bears fruit ten months of the year, and so one can reasonably expect to find fruit at almost any time. The time sequence regarding fig trees is this: first, the tree would have three years to grow after planting. The fruit of the next three years is considered forbidden (see Lev 19:23). The fruit of the seventh year is considered clean and ought to be offered to the Lord (Lev 19:24).

The owner in this parable has come seeking fruit for three years, hence it is nine years since planting, and the situation begins to look hopeless. He rightly urges that it be rooted out, but the gardener urges "mercy," give the tree yet another chance.

Keep in mind that the parable is not about trees but about the nation's leadership. The gardener's proposed remedy for the tree's problems reflects Jesus' mastery of "insult humor." Throughout the Gospels Jesus, the authentic Mediterranean native, resorts to insults on a regular basis, and they are always gems. The gardener might have proposed new soil for the tree, or increased watering. Instead he proposed spreading manure on it. Jesus' original peasant audience undoubtedly roared with laughter. This is just what those #)%!@* leaders need!

Moreover, in Aramaic there is a wordplay between "dig it out" and "let it alone" (also the word for forgiveness), which makes the parable and its point very easy to remember. Judgment (dig it out)? No, mercy and forgiveness (let it alone)! The tree cannot lift itself by its roots. They (the leaders) need the intervention of an outsider, the gardener, God himself!

Dedicated reformers are often so focused on the evils to be exterminated that they neglect the need for personal reform as well. This is as true of all as it is of leaders. This is the point Luke's Jesus makes in today's masterful cluster of readings. The passage is beautifully appropriate to Lent. It needs no further comment.

Fourth Sunday of Lent
Luke 15:1-3, 11-32

The parable of the two lost sons (vv. 11–32) is Jesus' self-justification for "hosting" sinners at table fellowship (vv 1–2).

The younger son (vv. 11–24). Fathers were discouraged from distributing inheritance during their lifetime (Sir 33:20-24). But if he did, a father still was entitled to live off the proceeds while he lived. This son acts shamefully, effectively wishing his father were dead. That the father did not explode and discipline him on the spot testifies to the depth of his love.

The elder son is no better. Instead of protesting the inappropriate property division and refusing his share, he accepts it (v. 12). And he makes no effort to reconcile his father and brother as culture demanded that he should. His behavior is equally shameful.

The younger son sinks deeper into shame. Selling his share of the family wealth infuriates his village neighbors (see 1 Kgs 21:3). Losing his money to non-Judeans through wasteful spending in a far-off land makes things worse. When the famine comes, he begins to starve.

In desperation, he tries to leech on to a wealthy patron, who in turn hopes to repel him by assigning a repulsive job. To the amazement of all, this Judaic lad agrees to feed pigs.

Still he starves. The carob pods fed to the pigs were the wild variety with bitter berries, nauseating and insufficiently nourishing to humans. Even though entitled to a share of butchered animals, the Judaic boy could not eat this forbidden food.

Motivated by his severe hunger, he regrets having lost the money (vv. 17–19). Not only can he no longer support himself, but he is also unable now to care for his father in old age. This he deeply regrets.

His solution? He resolves to become a "hired servant" of his family, thereby regaining a measure of honor, independence, and a social status equal to his brother and father. Moreover, he will be able to pay back what he lost, that is, he will be able to take care of his father for as long as the father lives.

He is willing to accept the shameful fact that the village will disown, reject, and physically abuse him for taking inheritance from the father before his death and then losing it to Gentiles, that is, non-Judeans (See Sir 26:5). He judges this a small price to pay for life and food.

The father then acts totally out of cultural character. He runs (very inappropriate for an elder) the gauntlet the village has prepared for the returning wayward son. He publicly forgives the son by kissing him again and again on the cheeks, and heals the broken relationship between them.

The best robe is certainly the father's. It will guarantee the son's acceptance by the community at the banquet. The signet ring indicates enormous trust. The sandals are a sign of being a free man in the house, not a servant. By placing sandals on his feet, the servants signal their reacceptance of him as son. Killing the calf means the entire village will be invited and prodded toward forgiveness. This size animal can feed more than one hundred people.

The elder son (vv. 25–32). Instead of honoring his father by accepting his brother and playing his appropriate role as chief host at the meal, the elder son publicly insults and humiliates his father (vv. 28–30).

The insults are jarring: he addresses his father without a respectful title; he speaks of himself as "slave" and not son (29); he accuses the father of favoritism (him a calf, me not even a goat!); he refuses to acknowledge his brother ("this son of yours"); he invents the claim that his brother lived with harlots. In effect, this elder son's heart has always been elsewhere. He, too, wishes his father were already dead.

Once again the father replies to a wayward son with love in acts of self-humiliation. He returns the insult with an endearing "my child. . . ." He assures him that his inheritance remains intact, and he invites the son to join the festivities.

Here the parable ends, rather abruptly.

What did the elder son do? That is the question the Pharisees and scribes (see Luke 15:2) and the modern believer must answer. What would you do?

Fifth Sunday of Lent
John 8:1-11

From a cultural perspective, at least two issues leap out of today's reading. What is adultery? On what basis is Jesus asked to judge this case?

ADULTERY

In the Mediterranean world the key figure in adultery is the wife (the married woman), and the key issue is loss of honor, or shame for the husband (see Sir 23:22-27). Women are believed to be intensely oversexed and therefore to require the constant vigilance of the key man in their lives: father over his daughter (Sir 42:9-10), brother over his sister (2 Sam 13:7-39), husband over his wife (Sir 26:1-9).

If a husband suspects adultery, he can put his wife through the "trial by ordeal" (see Num 5:11-31; it may have been this trial to which Joseph did not want to subject Mary in Matt 1:19). If adultery can be proven (Deut 22:22), both partners are to be killed.

Today's reading is interesting in that the guilty woman is said to have been caught in the act of intercourse, but her partner appears to have escaped. Deuteronomy 19:15 requires two witnesses to the fact, not including the husband, and apparently at least two witnesses trapped this poor woman.

In the light of this background, what culturally plausible scenario helps understand the event? Did the husband know of his wife's failures and set the trap, knowing full well she'd have to be killed? Or was he being cuckolded and did his enemies set the trap to further shame him? It is impossible to decide, but the embarrassment of the situation is surpassed only by the malice involved in setting the trap to catch the partners in the very act.

JESUS AS JUDGE

In John 8:15, Jesus claims: "I judge no one," yet in 8:26 he states: "I have much to say about you and much to judge." Scholars recognize these two statements as stemming from two different traditions separated by a considerable amount of time.

The question in this story of the woman caught in adultery is: Why did the Pharisees and scribes bring her to Jesus? How was he perceived to be competent to judge? The most likely answer is that Jesus was definitely perceived by others as a prophet and therefore competent to pronounce God's judgment. An editorial comment in verse 6 tells us of their base motive: it was to trap him so that he could be brought to trial.

There is a tradition that about the year 30 the Romans took away from the Sanhedrin the right of capital punishment. This is why they could not put Jesus to death. While it is impossible to tell whether this arrangement was in effect when this woman was caught, the most credible reason for involving Jesus in this matter is to assume that the arrangement already existed.

The trap is a dilemma. If Jesus urges that the woman be released, he clearly violates the Mosaic Law and proves himself to be an irreligious person. He is certainly no prophet. If he orders that she be stoned, he is in trouble with the Romans, who have taken this right away from the Judeans.

Jesus, as usual, is clever in wiggling out of the dilemma. He buys time for himself by doodling on the ground, a common custom among Mediterranean peasants when distraught. Finally, in response to the continual badgering by his opponents, Jesus challenges this overzealous lynch mob to examine their motives: "Let the one among you who is without sin—let that one be first to cast a stone at her."

This is not an argument against capital punishment. It rather questions the motives of the accusers. Perhaps the wronged husband has cynically prearranged to have his wife caught instead of trying to win her back with love (after the pattern of Hos 2:14-15). Perhaps the scribes and Pharisees are not interested primarily in the Law of Moses and its principles, or the woman's life situation, but rather in trapping Jesus.

Jesus the prophet, the one who speaks the will of God for the here-and-now, reminds them—and all zealots—to strive for purity of motive as they pursue their righteous goals.

Passion Sunday
Luke 22:14–23:56

In Mediterranean peasant culture of the past, achieving masculine identity is a life-long challenge. This is so because young boys are routinely brought up exclusively by the women and totally lack a male role model. Upon entering the harsh male world around the age of puberty, boys must learn to become men. One sign of manhood in this culture is the ability to bear physical punishment and pain without flinching or crying.

Hebrew Wisdom literature, particularly Proverbs and Sirach, served as the "Dr. Spock" books of their day. They repeatedly encourage fathers to punish their sons (never their daughters) physically. "He who loves his son will *whip* him often . . ." (Sir 30:1). *"Beat his ribs* while he is young, or else he will become stubborn and disobey you . . ." (Sir 30:12).

THEOLOGY AND HUMAN EXPERIENCE

Everything we know and say about God is rooted in and based upon our human experience. Culture plays a major role in shaping our human experience. The Mediterranean relationships between fathers and sons serve as their model for imagining how God would behave toward human beings and how the human being ought to respond.

Biblical heroes illustrate the point. Consider the obedient servant described by Isaiah who suffers undeservedly and in silence. "Like a lamb that is led to the slaughter, and like a sheep that before its shearer is silent, so he did not open his mouth" (Isa 53:7). "Yet it was the will of the Lord to crush him with pain" (v. 10). This servant and others, like the authors of laments in the book of Psalms (e.g., Psalm 22) who suffer innocently yet obediently to God's designs, served as models of proper, adult male behavior for youngsters.

THE PASSION OF JESUS

The Gospels portray Jesus as a very typical Mediterranean male. He is an obedient youngster. After returning from the pilgrimage to Jerusalem, "he went down with [his parents] and came to Nazareth, and was obedient to them" (Luke 2:51).

As an adult, Jesus is obedient to his heavenly Father. "Father, if you are willing, remove this cup from me; yet not my will, but yours be done" (Luke 22:42). (Recall that Luke omits this line from the Lord's Prayer in 11:2-4 and places it here for greater effect.)

Jesus imitated biblical heroes in his life. Luke and the other evangelists show this by drawing on Second Isaiah and on Psalms 22 and 69 in writing about Jesus. Luke's observation that "they cast lots to divide his clothing" is certainly borrowed from Psalm 22:18. The taunt of the leaders, "He saved others; let him save himself if he is the Messiah of God, his chosen one" (Luke 23:35) echoes Psalm 22:8. Jesus ranks among the finest biblical heroes who suffered in silence. The passion stories certainly make this point emphatically.

EPISTLE TO THE HEBREWS

The homilist who wrote this letter interpreted Jesus' passion this way: "*Because* he was a son, he learned obedience through what he suffered; and having been made perfect, he became the source of eternal salvation for all who obey him . . ." (Heb 5:8-10).

What does this mean for Christian believers who suffer? The homilist explains: "Endure trials for the sake of discipline. God is treating you as sons; for what son is there whom his father does not discipline? . . . We have had earthly fathers to discipline us, and we respected them. Should we not much more be subject to the Father of spirits and live? . . . God disciplines us for our good . . ." (read the entire passage, Heb 12:3-11).

AMERICAN BELIEVERS

There are at least two cultural challenges in today's Scripture reading and the mystery Christians celebrate. One is to read an accurate translation of the ancient texts. Inclusive language translations that omit "son" in the Hebrews passages as offensive to modern women and replace it with the plural "children" misrepresent Mediterranean culture and the Bible, which neither states nor implies that girls should be physically punished, and they unwittingly give permission to contemporaries who use the Bible as warrant for behavior to physically punish girls as well as boys.

The second challenge is how to translate a value or behavior from one culture in which it is acceptable and normal to another culture in which the same value or behavior is considered an abuse. Experts in human violence observe that every form of known family violence is acceptable in some cultures but considered abuse in others.

In this passion story Luke definitely proposes Jesus as a model to follow and imitate. This challenges modern believers to reconsider the biblical image and their image of God, God's will, suffering, suffering innocently, response to suffering, and related ideas. It still remains for all of us to devise appropriate ways to follow and imitate the Mediterranean Jesus that are in harmony with values Western culture considers humane.

Easter Sunday
John 20:1-9

In 1984 the Boston College biblical scholar, Pheme Perkins, wrote, "The theological task of articulating the significance of resurrection for twentieth-century Christians still remains to be undertaken" (*Resurrection*, Doubleday, p. 30). Despite her own and many fine publications since then, her judgment still stands. The grossly inaccurate discussion of this topic by journalists in *Time, Newsweek,* and *US News and World Report* at Easter time in 1995 suggested that even as scholars increasingly make their research available to the public, the message still needs to be more clearly articulated.

Scholars are agreed that Jesus' resurrection is *not* at all a miraculous return from the dead or something like a near-death experience. The real differences in the reports and interpretations of the evangelists and other New Testament authors make it quite clear that there is *no, single, unified picture* of resurrection in the tradition.

From this perspective, it is very significant that the gospel passage assigned for this great feast of Easter, John 20:1-9, is the story of the finding of the *empty tomb!* None of the resurrection appearances of Jesus was selected.

One purpose of the empty-tomb tradition is to remind believers that faith comes from hearing. John's report that the Beloved Disciple "sees" (the empty tomb and folded wrappings) and "believes" (that Jesus has been raised rather than that his corpse has been stolen) seems to replace the angelic proclamation in other accounts that "the Lord is risen!"

Mary Magdalene represents the community grieving over Jesus' death and needing consolation. Her report that "they" have stolen the body very likely refers to enemies of Jesus but could also reflect the community's concern about the charge that some *Messianists* stole the body to support their tale that Jesus was raised from the dead.

The early Peter tradition is of no help because, according to that report, he came to the tomb, found it empty, and returned to his friends without any understanding of what had happened (Luke 24:12). In John's report Peter enters the empty tomb first, and then the Beloved Disciple's reaction interprets what they both saw.

In this gospel passage, faith in the resurrection of Jesus developed from the discovery of an empty tomb and not from an appearance of Jesus. It developed from what the first believers reported and how they interpreted what they experienced.

TWENTIETH-CENTURY CHRISTIANS

Older believers probably remember the days before Vatican II when Catholic education regularly included a course called "apologetics," or "how to defend or prove the faith to nonbelievers and skeptics." We learned and memorized philosophical arguments to "prove" our beliefs, including our faith that Jesus rose from the dead.

The Second Vatican Council unleashed wave upon wave of fresh scholarship that improved our knowledge and demonstrated how overly simplistic our apologetics was. For instance, new Bible translations that correctly rendered the passages that proclaimed that "Jesus was raised [by God] from the dead" surprised us. We had never noticed this before.

As our knowledge of the ancient world and its culture grew and continues to grow, we realize that the Christian claims to have "salvation in Jesus" do not seem to satisfy the modern quest for meaning and well-being in a psychologically oriented and technologically blessed (and cursed) world.

Perhaps one piece of the biblical record can help us. The scriptural evidence suggests that the risen Jesus was somehow different, "transformed" (Mark 16:12) and somewhat unrecognizable (Luke 24:16; John 20:14; 21:14), though he was the same Jesus of Nazareth that had lived and walked on earth. These seem to be two constant elements that believers report in the appearances of the risen Jesus to them in an altered state of consciousness. Both elements characterize experiences of alternate realities in all cultures, so they are not really surprising. As each report indicates, the experience is reassuring and enlightening, quite in accord with the cultural function of such altered state-of-consciousness experiences.

The funeral liturgy reminds Christians that they shall experience this same transformation. In death "life is changed, not taken away." This echoes Paul's view: "So it is with the resurrection of the dead. What is sown is perishable, what is raised is imperishable. It is sown in dishonor, it is raised in honor. It is sown in weakness, it is raised in power. It is sown a physical body, it is raised a spiritual body" (1 Cor 15:42-44).

Today's feast and Christian belief in the resurrection of Jesus challenge all, scholar and nonscholar alike, to explore new ways of showing that belief in Jesus as God's definitive act of salvation truly gives ultimate purpose and meaning to life in our time.

Second Sunday of Easter
John 20:19-31

Poor Thomas! Branded forever with the adjective "doubting" in a story that scholars agree is a creation of John the evangelist. Thomas is made to typify the "doubts," skepticism, and hesitation that plagued all the early witnesses to the risen Jesus.

DOUBT IN THE MIDDLE EAST

Secrecy, deception, and lying are so common and prevalent in day-to-day life in the Middle East of past and present that every native entertains a healthy skepticism about everything. While a native Missourian insists that people who make mind-boggling claims should "show me!" thus implying that "seeing is believing," natives of the Middle East would not agree.

Remember the parable of Lazarus and the greedy man (Luke 16:19-31)? When the greedy man experiences the punishment that his lifestyle has merited for him in eternity, he begs father Abraham to send Lazarus back to his surviving brothers to warn them. Abraham replies: "If they do not listen to Moses and the prophets [that is, believe the Scripture that they read or hear], neither will they be convinced even if someone rises from the dead."

What, then, is the purpose of the Thomas episode?

THOMAS THE APOSTLE

The name "Thomas" is a Greek transliteration of the Hebrew word *to'am*, which means "twin." Greek-speaking Christians would not understand "Thomas" but would certainly understand its Greek translation, "Didymus," Thomas probably was not a "twin" in the modern sense but was rather given this name to distinguish him from another person with the same name as his. One tradition *(Acts of Thomas)* assigns him the then common Judean name of "Judas Thomas," so that "Thomas" or "Didymus" would identify him as "the other Judas."

The Fourth Gospel provides scattered glimpses of his personality. In John 11:16 he stands out among the disciples as a strong man, willing to go with Jesus into hostile Judea even if it should mean the death of both of them (11:7). At the same time, this passage also hints that he is a disbeliever in what has happened and will happen with Mary and Martha's brother, Lazarus.

At the Last Supper, Thomas admits a certain lack of understanding (14:5) about Jesus and his destiny. In the dark garden Thomas apparently joins the others who "forsook Jesus and fled" (Mark 14:59). In many ways, then, Thomas is no better or different from his fellow apostles.

THOMAS' DOUBT

Would Thomas be offended to know that the evangelist created a story featuring him as a "doubter"? Probably not. This characterization is quite in accord with what is known of him in John 11:16 and 14:5. Some think that he may indeed have been with the group in 20:19 when the risen Jesus appeared and that Thomas initially didn't believe his eyes.

At this appearance Jesus showed the disciples his hands and his side (v. 20). This action was most definitely intended to dispel their unspoken but very real doubts and to assure them (and us) that this person is not a ghost but the self-same Jesus of Nazareth who was crucified and died on the cross. For these disciples, it seems that seeing is believing. No one asks to touch and verify the wounds.

Thomas presents a contrast. He wants to physically probe Jesus' body to confirm the miraculous. Yet when confronted with Jesus invitation to touch him (v. 27), Thomas backs off.

He rapidly comes to his senses and confesses his faith: "My Lord and My God." He accepts Jesus' new invitation: "Do not persist in your disbelief, but become a believer."

BELIEVING WITHOUT SEEING

Writing for a later generation of Messianists who were gradually being deprived of apostolic witnesses by death, John composed the story of Thomas and the "beatitude" that concludes today's episode: "Truly worthy of esteem are those who have not seen and yet have believed."

Just as Thomas and his fellow apostles were able to make a significant cultural leap and suspend their suspicions of deception to believe what they saw, so too, modern, scientific-minded Christians who no longer have anything to see must believe what they hear. Paul reminds us that "faith comes from hearing" (Rom 10:17).

Third Sunday of Easter
John 21:1-19

Peter's threefold affirmative reply to Jesus' thrice-repeated question, "Simon Son of John, do you love me more than these?" (John 21:15, 16, 17) is correctly seen as Peter's atonement for his triple denial of Jesus (John 18:15-18, 25-27). But it is more than that.

COMPETITION AMONG DISCIPLES

In the ancient and contemporary Middle East leaders gather followers and form factions for the purpose of gaining some advantage over others. Those who follow a leader know and understand full well what the leader is after. They join the leader because they believe that in unity there is strength, that this group together can achieve more and achieve it more effectively than any individual might do alone. Each group member is strongly bonded with the leader.

In contrast, group members have weak bonds to each other. It is no surprise that James and John, the sons of Zebedee, ask for the two highest places when Jesus comes into his glory (Mark 10:35-37), and that the other ten become angry because these two beat them to the punch (v. 41). Even at the Last Supper they all dispute among themselves about status and honor and "which one of them was to be regarded as the greatest" (Luke 22:24).

In John's Gospel the Beloved Disciple stands out rather clearly as particularly favored by Jesus. He reclines next to

Jesus at table (13:23) and obtains privileged information from him about the betrayer (13:25-26). Even Peter doesn't know this and has to use the Beloved Disciple as an intermediary to get to Jesus (13:24).

PETER AND THE BELOVED DISCIPLE

There is a definite contrast between Peter and the Beloved Disciple in John's Gospel. The Beloved Disciple appears to be superior to Peter. When he describes the noble shepherd (John 10:1-18), Jesus notes that the shepherd "enters by the door" (v. 2). Moreover, the gatekeeper confirms the identity of the shepherd: "He who enters by the door is the shepherd of the sheep. To him the gatekeeper opens."

The noble shepherd also leads the sheep in and out. "He calls his own sheep by name and leads them out. When he has brought out all his own, he goes before them, and the sheep follow him" (vv. 3–4).

The evangelist John uses this very imagery to describe the Beloved Disciple. After Jesus was arrested, he was taken to the high priest. Here, the Beloved Disciple, who was known to the high priest, *entered* "with Jesus into the courtyard of the high priest, but Peter was *standing outside the gate*" (18:15). Then this other disciple, "who was known to the high priest, went out, spoke to the woman who guarded the gate, and brought Peter in" (John 18:16). Clearly, the Beloved Disciple is portrayed as a noble shepherd because (1) he enters by the door, (2) the gatekeeper (woman) recognizes him, and (3) he leads the sheep in. Peter is not the shepherd, he is a lowly sheep!

PETER, FROM HIRELING TO SHEPHERD

If one rereads the contrast of the noble shepherd and the hireling in John 10, Peter is portrayed by the evangelist as a hireling. He lacks knowledge of the traitor; he needs the Beloved Disciple to gain entrance to the high priest's court. In abandoning Jesus he behaves like a hireling rather than a disciple. He denies Jesus, and even after the resurrection, he runs slower than the Beloved Disciple, sees but does not say anything (John 20:4-9).

The episode in which Peter three times affirms his love for Jesus is a turning point in the Gospel, even though scholars recognize this chapter (21) as an "appendix" produced not by the evangelist but by his circle of followers. In this episode Peter is explicitly acclaimed by Jesus to be the shepherd of the flock. Peter firmly professes his loyalty to the Lord. And the Beloved Disciple bows out of the picture in the next few verses (20–23) without saying another word.

Insights from Mediterranean culture highlight how untidy and confusing the early circle of believers really was. Competition was rife; this was culturally normal. But no matter how intently others jockeyed for position, or how well the Beloved Disciple played the role of noble shepherd, it is Jesus the leader who makes the final decision: Peter is appointed noble shepherd.

Fourth Sunday of Easter
John 10:27-30

Viewed in their cultural context, these brief verses presuppose an intimate and detailed knowledge of two key elements: the relationship of a Mediterranean father and son, and the Mediterranean understanding of sheep and shepherds.

MEDITERRANEAN FATHERS AND SONS

Though brought up from birth exclusively by the women, a Mediterranean boy at the age of puberty is brusquely shoved into the hierarchical and harsh world of the men. Here he learns obedience and manliness, commonly by being taught to stoically endure physical punishment.

John the evangelist portrays the relationship of Jesus and his heavenly Father in terms of an authentic and perfect Mediterranean relationship between father and son. The heavenly Father loves Jesus (3:5), and Jesus knows his Father intimately (8:55; 10:15). Jesus was taught by his Father (8:22) and does the will of the Father (4:34; 6:38). Uniquely in John's Gospel, Jesus has received a command from his Father that concerns his death and resurrection: "I have power to lay [my life] down, and to take it up again. I have received this command from my Father" (10:18). Jesus obeys this command unquestioningly, perfectly, stoically.

How are Jesus and the Father "one"? In power and activity, a perfectly intelligible conclusion that can be logically drawn from the ideal relationship they share as Father and

Son from a Mediterranean cultural perspective. Jesus does what the Father empowers him to do. Jesus can do what the Father does: safeguard the sheep of the flock.

MEDITERRANEAN MEN AND SHEEP

As in every culture, so too in the Mediterranean world, animals are interpreted and treated as symbols of the internal differences peculiar to this world. The Mediterranean world is driven by the value of honor. Honor is associated with men, who must protect and maintain it even to the point of death. If the risk of death is involved, the honorable man will suffer it in silence, without complaint.

Mediterranean people noticed that this was also how sheep behaved. While being shorn or even being prepared for slaughter, the sheep remains silent and does not cry. This is how Isaiah describes the ideal servant of the Lord: "like a lamb that is led to the slaughter, and like a sheep that before its shearers is silent, so [the servant] did not open his mouth" (Isa 53:7). It is only natural for the Mediterranean native to associate men with sheep. Sheep therefore are animals that symbolize honor.

Shepherds, however, are a different matter. In history, they were considered noble, honorable figures. The prophet Ezekiel (34) referred to kings as "shepherds." God was viewed by pious Judeans as a shepherd (Psalm 23). But in first-century day-to-day life they were considered unclean, one reason being that they often violated the property rights of others in pasturing their sheep. Another reason was that long absences from home made it impossible for them to protect the womenfolk as they ought. Hence the shameful reputation of shepherds in the first century.

By calling himself the "noble shepherd," Jesus aligns himself with kings, and even with God, his Father. By calling his followers "sheep," he recognizes their honorable status.

In today's reading, Jesus highlights three honorable activities of a shepherd on behalf of his sheep. (1) The shepherd knows his sheep very well and not like a hireling who could care less. (2) He keeps them safe from violent attack ("no one [human or beast] shall snatch them out of his hand"). (3) The Noble Shepherd, Jesus, gives his followers life everlasting ("they shall never perish").

As an honorable Mediterranean man carefully looks after his friends, and as an honorable Mediterranean shepherd tends the sheep of the flock, so Jesus and his Father look after those who hear their voice and follow them.

AMERICANS, FATHERS, AND SHEEP

American views of father-and-son relationships are radically different from Mediterranean views. Moreover, Americans in general and American Christians in particular do not like to be compared with sheep. Americans believe, rather, in self-reliance. Appreciating John's presentation of Jesus and his Father in today's Scripture poses a challenge to American believers, but they cannot escape it if they wish to be Christians. How would you translate the passage?

Fifth Sunday of Easter
John 13:31-35

Once again, a few brief verses from Scripture presume a broader and deeper understanding of its Mediterranean cultural context. Specifically, this selection from Jesus' farewell address to his disciples (see Jacob's farewell addresses to his sons in Gen 47:29–49:33) urges further reflection upon honor (= "glory") and upon the "newness" of the love-command.

GLORY: GOD'S HONOR

In Mediterranean culture honor is a public claim to worth or value *and* a public recognition and acknowledgment of that claim. What is Jesus' claim to worth in this passage? The subject is his imminent death. By obeying the command of his father (10:18) concerning his death, Jesus can claim the honor of an obedient son.

Further, the stoic acceptance of death validates his claim to Mediterranean manliness and marks him as a son who learned his father's lessons well. In addition, Jesus claims to have the personal power to lay down his life and pick it up again (10:18), an honorable power granted him by the Father. Thus does Jesus demonstrate his personal honor, and thus also does he honor his Father.

The Father's honor-claim is closely bound up with Jesus, the Son. God the Father is honored by his Son's spontaneous and unquestioning obedience even unto death. But God's greatest honor-claim resides in raising the Son from the dead. This powerful action totally reverses the shameful dimension of the crucifixion and demonstrates that God did not abandon his Son, a just person, to eternal shame and oblivion, but rather endowed him with an honor that no one else could bestow: risen life.

AMERICANS AND HONOR

Generally speaking, Americans are unmoved by considerations of honor and shame. Disgraced elected or corporate officials seem unaffected by shame and often manage to move on to bigger, better, and still more profitable levels. Shamed athletes are still proposed for membership in their respective American hall of "honor." Even at the service academies where honor is an expressly professed value, flagrant infractions have become common. And when culprits are caught and charged, they hire attorneys for defense. In honor cultures, going to court and hiring an attorney is shameful and an admission of defeat (Prov 25:7-10; Luke 12:57-59). For Americans, the notion of honor carries nowhere near the importance that it does in the Mediterranean world.

How, then, can American believers appreciate what John the evangelist writes about Jesus and his Father in today's Scripture? They must strive to see life from *the evangelist's* Mediterranean point of view. Without an understanding of honor as a core cultural value, the meaning of "glory" and "glorification" is completely lost.

THE "NEW" COMMANDMENT

Other farewell addresses in the Bible and other ancient literature usually exhort the survivors, the "children," to practice moral virtue or to remain obedient to the Law. Jesus' farewell address lays down a "love command," which is described as "new." "I give you a new commandment, that you love one another" (13:34).

The "newness" of this command is difficult to specify. In his farewell address to Esau and Jacob, Isaac commanded: "Be loving of your brothers as a man loves himself, with each man seeking for his brother what is good for him . . . loving each other as themselves" (*Jubilees* 36:4-5). Similar sentiments are also found in the New Testament (1 Thess 4:9; Rom 13:9; Gal 5:14; Mark 12:31).

What is evident in all these passages (including John 13:34) is that love is extended only to other members of the inner circle, the community, and not to those outside. "By this everyone [else, outside] will know that you are my disciples [insiders], if you have love for one another" (John 13:35). This example of mutual love among insiders should be a stirring example to all outsiders.

The best explanation for the "newness" of Jesus' commandment is implied in the themes that are woven throughout the farewell address: intimacy, indwelling, mutual knowledge. These are the themes that characterize a covenant, in this case, the "new" covenant struck at the Last Supper. God's covenantal love is spontaneous, unmotivated, directed to sinners and others unworthy of love. Israel experienced this love of old (Deut 7:6-8). In Jesus' death and resurrection, God's love is known in a totally new dimension.

AMERICANS AND THE "NEW" COMMANDMENT

To the credit of its basically individualistic culture, Americans do "love one another" but in culturally distinctive ways. For example, Americans invented the curious distinction between the "deserving" and the "undeserving" poor. Love is directed accordingly. In contrast, Jesus urges, "Just as I have loved you, you also should love one another" (13:34). How do we measure up?

Sixth Sunday of Easter
John 14:23-29

Modern Christians live comfortably with the theological precision honed over twenty centuries of investigation, debate, and sometimes heated disagreements. They rarely realize how much turmoil and confusion their ancestors experienced in the first century.

DEATH OF THE APOSTLES

The first believers cherished the presence of the apostolic eyewitnesses to the life, ministry, and message of Jesus. As a living link to Jesus, these witnesses were able to interpret and apply the teachings of Jesus to new situations in which the community found itself.

When the apostles began to die, believers felt the loss. For John's community, the death of the Beloved Disciple (probably just before the Fourth Gospel was given its final form around A.D. 90) was a severe blow felt very personally. Who would help them now?

DESTRUCTION OF JERUSALEM

After a four-year war, the Roman armies led by Titus destroyed Jerusalem and the Temple in the year 70. Judeans and Messianists were both deeply affected. Judeans lost more than a beloved monument. They lost God's special dwelling place among them, the key place where God could be encountered in their liturgies.

Messianists had expected that Jesus' return would accompany God's wrathful judgment on the city of Jerusalem. But Jesus did not return on that occasion, and as years passed expectation of his speedy return began to pale. The death of the Beloved Disciple also heightened frustration relative to Jesus' return because he was one of those who was expected to be alive until that time (John 21:22; see also Mark 13:30; Matt 10:23). If Jesus is not yet returning, who will help believers now?

THE PARACLETE

Scholars conclude that the concept of the "paraclete" is an answer to this question. In the absence of living eyewitnesses to Jesus and with the increased delay of Jesus' return, the "paraclete" will guide and help believers.

Modern sophisticated Christians know that the "Paraclete" is the "Holy Spirit." Our earliest ancestors in the Faith, the first-century Christians of John the evangelist's community, were less precise in their understanding. Jesus is the paraclete in 1 John 2:1, and the Holy Spirit is the paraclete in John 16:7. These passages suggest that the word is best understood as describing a function rather than serving as a name or title in the Johannine writings.

What is this function? The variety of translations found in modern Bibles indicates how difficult that question is to answer. The English word "paraclete" simply transliterates the Greek word that basically means "advocate." This word has legal connotation. Literally it means "one who stands by the side of a defendant."

The 1956 *Jerusalem Bible* translates paraclete as "advocate," but the 1985 *Jerusalem Bible* uses "paraclete!" The 1970 *New American Bible* translation used "paraclete," but the 1986 revision replaced it with "advocate!" Other translations prefer the word "counselor" *(New International Version)* or "comforter"*(King James Version)*.

What does the evangelist himself indicate the meaning might be? The "paraclete" performs at least three functions or activities. (1) It is the continued presence of Jesus on earth after Jesus' departure to heaven (14:12, 16). (2) It is a truth-telling spirit (14:17; 16:13) that testifies on behalf of Jesus and in defense of him. It affirms that Jesus was not a shameful failure but rather the beloved of God, a faithful and dutiful Son. (3) It reminds them of things that Jesus said (14:26) and reveals things Jesus was unable to convey (16:12-14). The "paraclete," therefore, represents divine presence and guidance for the early Messianists.

It is very likely that modern Western believers experience difficulty appreciating the exasperation our ancestors in the Faith would experience without a "paraclete" as just described. After all, we vigorously defend our individual "right to know." The ancient world was shot through with secrecy and deception. If anything, they believed that no one had a right to know.

In addition, we are confident even as individuals that we can get to the bottom of things. We have legal recourse by means of the "freedom of information act." In the ancient world, if you didn't have an "inside source," or a "paraclete," you were certainly "not in the know."

Jesus' guarantee that the Father will give his followers a paraclete gives them enormous peace, and "not as the world gives peace" (14:27). Even we can now see why.

Seventh Sunday of Easter
John 17:20-26

Internationally known biblical scholar Raymond Brown followed up his masterful two-volume commentary on the Gospel of John with a book entitled *The Community of the Beloved Disciple: The Life, Loves, and Hates of an Individual Church in New Testament Times* (Paulist Press, 1979). Readers familiar with John's Gospel know only too well how easy it is to identify those whom John and his community "hate."

One conclusion scholars correctly draw about John's community is that it is recently broken away or ejected from existing Judean institutions. It has become an entity unto itself, strongly committed to the God of Israel, who is immediately accessible in and through Jesus. The situation John's Gospel reflects is "them" versus "us," or "insiders" versus "outsiders."

Keeping this in mind, today's selection from Jesus' prayer at the Last Supper (John 17:1-26) raises this question: "For whom and what does Jesus pray when he asks 'that *all* may be one'?" (v. 21).

UNITY OF BELIEVERS

John's Jesus very pointedly prays for the "insiders," that is, for his disciples and for those "who will believe in me through their word" (v. 20). It was also the "insiders" who received the new commandment "to love one another" (13:34).

A key element in both passages (17:21 and 13:34), however, is that Jesus serves as the model. Disciples ought to love one another to the degree that Jesus loves those who believe in him: to the point of death. The community of believers in Jesus ought to strive for unity like that which exists between Jesus and the Father.

DIVINE INITIATIVE

That Jesus prays to the Father for this unity very clearly demonstrates its origins. The unity he desires is not the result of harmonious human interaction, or the end product of a human growth-and-development seminar. No, unity is a gift that flows down from the Father and Son to believers. It is precisely the organic and vital unity of the Father and Son that Jesus wants to communicate to believers.

LOVE: ORGANICALLY VITAL AND VISIBLE

Sometimes community can be a stifling and suffocating experience. Perhaps individualistically oriented Americans are more sensitive to this than people of other cultures. The organic unity of believers ought to be life-giving rather than death-dealing (see John 6:57). Community ought to enrich life's meaning rather than suck meaning out of individual life.

Moreover, true to the public nature of Mediterranean culture, this life and love of a believing community must be visible to others, especially the hostile group generically identified in this Gospel as "the world." There ought be no hiding the light of love under a bushel.

THE LOVING COMMUNITY

The proper response to this gift of life and unity from Father and Son is mutual love among members of the community. Outsiders will be amazed and moved (or motivated) by what they see. "By this [all the outsiders] will know you are my disciples, if you have love for one another" (13:35).

This is not to say that "the world" will automatically be converted or resolve to make a positive decision relative to

Jesus. Rather, "the world" will receive from the community what Jesus himself gave: a challenge to recognize God in him, God's pleasure with his behavior, and God's approving action on his behalf in the resurrection. Only such a mighty act of God could effectively undo the shame of the crucifixion. Believers, like Jesus, must keep the challenge ever before nonbelievers.

ECUMENISM

Brown notes that the seeming hostility of John's group to other Christian churches is really only apparent. "Us" included Christians who did not share the specifics of belief about Jesus that John's group held. They very likely were more inclusive than one might think at first glance.

Modern Christians, especially since Vatican II, have redoubled their efforts to promote unity among all Christian groups. Ecumenism has even encouraged more kindly approaches toward and commitments to understanding non-Christian religious groups. If Christians meet the challenge of Jesus' Last Supper prayer and its implications, their ecumenical activities stand a better chance of bearing fruit.

Pentecost
John 20:19-23

Americans hold ambivalent opinions about leaders. While they readily applaud good leaders, they are never quite certain how to identify and certify good candidates for leadership. Endorsements by influential figures or organizations no longer seem to carry much weight. Unfounded rumors and sensational reports in tabloids seem to be more important.

AUTHENTICATING A LEADER

Our Mediterranean ancestors in the Faith took a different view of leaders and leadership. For one, a legitimate leader had to be suitably "installed" as leader. Today's gospel narrative contains the major elements of a "vocation commissioning" event, a literary form that is commonly used in the Bible to authenticate different kinds of leaders.

Introduction. Confronting bewildered disciples in a locked room, Jesus reassures them with a word ("Peace!") and a gesture (displays his pierced hands and side). He is not a ghost but is alive, risen!

Commission. Jesus commissions the disciples after the pattern of his own commissioning by the Father. The commission is (1) formal (v. 21); (2) sealed by the gift of the Holy Spirit (v. 22); and (3) involves preaching repentance and forgiveness of sins (v. 23).

In John's Gospel, sin is the failure to believe in Jesus as the One the Father has sent. Hence this commission is best interpreted as charging these new leaders to bring new members into the community. It differs from the traditional understanding of forgiveness of sin in Matthew 18:19, which describes how the community deals with the sinfulness of its present members.

IDENTIFYING CREDIBLE LEADERS

In the Mediterranean world, a person who has a grievance realizes that personal efforts by an individual acting alone are futile. Only groups wield power, hence an aggrieved person gathers a group of sympathetic followers who have similar grievances. Such a group is called a faction. This group of aggrieved individuals believe that only by acting in unison will they be able to accomplish that which is impossible for a single one of them to accomplish alone. From a cultural viewpoint, this is the most plausible explanation for the way the Mediterranean artisan Jesus called and attracted his followers.

In the gospel story line, Jesus established and strengthened his credibility by winning every argument with his opponents. No matter how often people try to trick him or trip him up, he comes out on top. His honorable reputation and his credibility grows, and he is never shamed . . .

Until his death. Crucified just like and between two common criminals, Jesus suddenly seems to be overcome by the deepest possible cultural shame . . . until his resurrection. Then it becomes clear that God is indeed pleased with this beloved Son, for by raising him from the dead God has honored him far more than any human accolades ever could.

All these ideas stand behind Jesus' statement "As the Father has sent me, so I send you."

THE POWER OF A LEADER

In the ancient and contemporary Mediterranean world, people believe in a huge, diverse, and very real spirit world. Apocryphal books contemporary with New Testament times identify and name scores of spirits: good, evil, and mischievous. Some of these books even prescribe remedies, formulas, and talismans for protection against them.

It is difficult for modern, scientifically minded Western believers to appreciate the conviction by our ancestors in the Faith that these spirits were very powerful for good and ill. Luke's Gospel, for instance, is filled with many references to diverse spirit activity: Mary becomes pregnant by the power of a spirit (1:35); Peter's mother-in-law suffers from a spirit named "Fever" (4:38); the stooped-over woman had a spirit of infirmity and was bound by the spirit Satan for eighteen years (13:16); and on and on.

That these newly commissioned disciples would be gifted with a very powerful spirit, the Holy Spirit (John 19:22), only guaranteed their efficaciousness. Any first- or second-century Mediterranean native who heard or read today's gospel verses would respect and accept these disciples as legitimate, honorable, and effective ministers commissioned by none other than Jesus, who had received from his Father the highest of honors: risen life.

Today's gospel challenges Americans to reconsider how they select and evaluate leaders, both spiritual and secular.

Trinity
John 16:12-15

It is impossible to overestimate the overwhelming importance of honor and the fear of shame in Mediterranean culture. Honor is more valuable than money. Indeed, it is the supreme wealth in this culture. Without honor, one might as well be dead.

It should be no surprise, then, to learn that in this culture secrecy, deception, and lying are legitimate strategies for maintaining honor and avoiding shame. As Peter's denial of Jesus shockingly demonstrates (see John 18:15-18, 25-27), it is preferable to lie and preserve honor—even for a moment—than to admit the truth and suffer shame.

Clearly the prevalence of secrecy, deception, and lying in this culture made life very exasperating. In an argument with enemies, the exasperated Jesus charges: "Why do you not understand what I say? . . . You are from your father the devil. . . . He is a liar, and the father of lies," to which they respond with a deliberate lie in order to counter his shaming accusation: "Are we not right in saying that you are a Samaritan and have a demon?" (John 8:43-48).

This false but perhaps frequent charge against Jesus explains his constant repetition in John's Gospel of the phrase "Amen, amen, (or truly, truly) I say to you. . . ." This phrase was a strategy for assuring listeners that a speaker was telling the truth.

PARACLETE: SPIRIT OF TRUTH

Only against the background of these Mediterranean cultural values does the role of a paraclete as "Spirit of truth" make sense. The Greek word "paraclete," sometimes inaccurately interpreted as "comforter or consoler," is more correctly translated as "mediator, intercessor, or helper." It is not a title of the Holy Spirit because Jesus, too, is a paraclete (see 1 John 2:1).

Recall the importance and utter reality of the spirit world in Mediterranean culture. When human efforts to arrive at the truth are continually thwarted by secrecy, lying, and deception, one can only hope for help from another source. Fortunately, Jesus points to the Paraclete, the Spirit of truth, as such a helper.

PARACLETE: GUIDE INTO ALL TRUTH

In John's Gospel, "truth" is belief in Jesus as the unique revelation of God and as the one who speaks the words of God (see 3:33; 8:40, 47). In a world filled with secrecy, deception, and lying–even about Jesus!–the prayer of the psalmist is ever more poignant: "Let your good spirit guide me on a level path!" The Paraclete is the answer to this prayer.

THINGS THAT ARE TO COME

Mediterranean culture has little if any awareness of a far-off future. Only God knows the distant future. An interpretation *(Pesher)* of Habakkuk 7:1-3 discovered at Qumran reports: "God told [the prophet] to write down 'the things that were to come,' but he did not tell them when that moment would come to fulfillment."

This culture is very solidly present-oriented; it is very much a "now" generation. Rather than the future, they speak of the "forthcoming." A baby is a "forthcoming" event quite evident in a pregnant mother.

Within this cultural context, what the Paraclete offers is sure guidance to the community in its ever-deepening understanding of Jesus as the fulfillment of everything that had been promised in Scripture.

THE "HONOR" OF JESUS

In the face of ever-present secrecy, lying, deception, false charges, and counter-charges, when honor is difficult to ascertain, how satisfying—in a culture where honor is the core value—to be assured by Jesus that the Paraclete will "glorify" him, that is, will announce his true honor. "He will take what is mine and declare it to you." The Paraclete will learn the honorable truth straight from the source and pass it along to believers.

American believers are understandably impatient with a value like honor that does not figure prominently in American culture. On the other hand, ongoing political experiences have made Americans very keenly aware of how difficult it is to attain the truth and how often they are lied to by leaders in many fields. Perhaps the lack of a paraclete in our culture, a sure guide to all the truth, stirs a better appreciation for the guarantee of a paraclete in Mediterranean culture.

Corpus Christi
Luke 9:11-17

Low-context literature leaves little to the imagination. For instance, the terms of a credit-card agreement are spelled out in great detail and in minuscule print. High-context literature, like comic strips and the Bible, leave much to the imagination. These authors respect the intelligence of their readers and trust they will supply the proper details.

Separated by centuries and culture from their Mediterranean ancestors in the Faith, American believers turn to cultural experts for help in filling in appropriate details of Bible stories such as today's gospel.

GEOGRAPHY

The feeding of the crowd takes place near Bethsaida ("house of fishing"), situated on the northern shore of the Sea of Galilee, east of the Jordan. It had been a village (Mark 8:26), but Herod Philip raised it to the status of a city and named it Julia in honor of Caesar Augustus' daughter. There may have been two locations for Bethsaida: a fishing village on the lakeshore and the "city" some miles inland. Jesus cursed Bethsaida because of its unbelief and failure to repent (Luke 10:13). A map would help a reader to construct an appropriate geographical scenario for this story.

Generally speaking, the area outside villages and cities was considered to be chaos or wilderness (see 2 Cor 11:26). This is a most unlikely place for any gathering, much less a meal, hence the setting of this event is very strange indeed.

POPULATION

What would a crowd of 5,000 men represent? Based on computer calculations of agricultural production in Palestine, the amount of food necessary for subsistence survival, and similar considerations, scholars estimate that the total population of first-century Palestine was probably around 250,000.

Relying on the technique of rank-size modeling, cities are estimated to have about 10,000 residents, towns in the 1,000s, villages in the 100s, and hamlets in the 10s. On the basis of population, first-century Palestine probably had about two or three cities (Jerusalem, Caesarea by the Sea), about 32 towns, 315 villages, and 350 hamlets. This hypothetical estimate is generally confirmed by the current archaeological record.

A crowd of 5,000 men, therefore, would represent half a city, 1 to 5 towns, 10 to 50 villages, or 100 to 500 hamlets. Matthew 14:21 tells us that this number (5,000) did not include women and children, thereby reporting that the crowd was even larger! In this case, as elsewhere in the Bible, the numbers seem to have more of a symbolic than a factual significance.

MEALS

The geographical world of our Mediterranean ancestors in the Faith was divided by gender into male space (e.g., the fields) and female space (e.g., the common oven, the kitchen). Both genders could be in common spaces (e.g., village square) but never together at the same time. This makes Luke's report that 5,000 *men* ate very plausible.

In the home men ate alone, and women and children ate separately and usually earlier. Only after boys passed the age of puberty and entered the male world did they join the men for meals. Matthew's comment about the women and children correlates well with the Mediterranean understanding of space. The groups of fifty into which Jesus directed they gather were very likely clustered by gender: men and boys past the age of puberty were in some groups; women and children (boys and girls) were in other groups.

Grain, oil, and wine were the three staples of this culture, with grain and its products—especially bread—being the most important. Bread provided about one-half the caloric intake of much of the ancient Mediterranean world, with wheat being considered superior to barley and sorghum, the food of the poor (see John 6:9).

Fish in Palestine did not become popular as a food until the first century, though it was difficult to obtain except near the Mediterranean coast and the Sea of Galilee.

INTERPRETATION

This is not a lakeside family picnic but rather a story about a mind-boggling gathering of people who live in chaos and whose daily fare was hardly more than a subsistence serving of food. Jesus ministers to all their needs with a warm welcome, uplifting teaching, compassionate healing, and sufficient physical nourishment for everyone with food to spare (twelve full baskets). The traditional eucharistic interpretation of this passage well accords with this cultural base.

Eleventh Sunday in Ordinary Time
Luke 7:36–8:3

Though similar to stories reported in Matthew 26:6-13, Mark 14:3-9, and John 12:1-8, Luke's report appears to be an independent tradition. Sensitivity to the cultural world in which this story originated makes it possible to highlight a few of Luke's special interests.

DEBT

The central point of this story—forgiveness of sin—hinges on first-century Mediterranean peasant understanding of debt. Scholars estimate that excessive claims upon meager peasant resources (tithes, taxes, tribute, numerous tolls) consumed between 35 and 40 percent of total agricultural production. The path to enormous indebtedness required but a few small steps.

Peasants who were unable to repay their loans lost their land and became tenant sharecroppers. When this, too, failed, they were driven from their ancestral land. Since the scriptural evidence indicates that Jesus was known by all to be from Nazareth yet his ancestral ties extended back to Bethlehem, scholars suggest that at some point in history his ancestors experienced precisely this kind of fate. Such dispossessed people who lost their land frequently became artisans like Joseph and Jesus.

It is this experience of material indebtedness and both the hope and possibility of its forgiveness as in Jesus' parable (and the Lord's Prayer) that helped a peasant to understand the forgiveness of sin. Jesus' question to Simon the Pharisee was easy to answer: a person forgiven a large debt would exhibit greater gratitude than someone forgiven a smaller debt.

Our ancestors typically judged each other by external features and actions (1 Sam 16:7). Anyone who witnessed the woman's uninhibited display of love and gratitude could conclude from her actions that she had already experienced forgiveness of sin. "Her many sins have surely been forgiven by God since she has shown such love."

THE MEAL

The traditional luxury meal had two stages. During the first stage as initial courses—appetizers, for example, flatbread and a variety of dips—were served, the servants would attend the guests, wash them, and anoint them with perfumed oils as a kind of deodorant. During the second stage the primary courses of the meal were served.

As this story unfolds, it is clear that the Pharisee is no friend of Jesus. In the ancient Mediterranean world men eat separately from women and children younger than the age of puberty. Only a widow is permitted to serve the men.

Simon appears to have taken no precautions to keep other women out of the dining area. He certainly does nothing to prevent the known sinner woman from approaching and touching Jesus. Proper and improper touching deals with purity, and purity laws relative to meals are particularly rigorous. Touching by an unclean woman is discussed in Leviticus 15:19-32. Jesus' suspected ignorance of the common local knowledge about this woman's status causes the Pharisee to express doubt in his mind that Jesus is a prophet. He should be very astute about the here and now.

But Jesus, like many prophets in the Bible, reads Simon's heart and mind (see John 4:19) and responds to what he is thinking but has not explicitly expressed. Simon seems still unimpressed.

THE WOMAN AND THE PHARISEE

Luke also paints a deliberate contrast between the Pharisee and the woman. By inviting Jesus to a meal, the Pharisee recognizes Jesus as an equal. In the Mediterranean world, only equals can invite each other to meals. But after Jesus' arrival, the Pharisee extends no other sign of hospitality, suggesting that he does not accept Jesus for who he is: God's prophet.

The woman stands in stark contrast. The story tells us she was a sinner but gives not a clue regarding the nature of her sin. Though her sinful reputation was known in the city, we do not know what city it was. That she boldly enters the men's space (reclining at table) and is not impeded by Simon suggests she might be a widow, but Simon's neglect may also be part of his determination to withhold signs of hospitality and respect for Jesus.

The woman, however, performs for Jesus all the signs of hospitality that the Pharisee quite intentionally omitted: she provides water for cleansing (v. 44), tenders a kiss of greeting (v. 45), and provides perfumed oil for anointing (v. 46). It is precisely these deeds that tell us the woman has been forgiven. Simon's refusal to act like a host indicates that he has not experienced–perhaps not even sought–forgiveness.

Contemporary Western commitments to equality as a cultural value often make it difficult to perceive other cultures respectfully on their own terms. In today's story, *what* the woman has done for Jesus is much more important than her alleged reputation or status.

Twelfth Sunday in Ordinary Time
Luke 9:18-24

The Mediterranean cultural world of the past and the present is rooted in honor as the core value. Honor is a public claim to worth and a public acknowledgment of that claim by others.

Acquired honor is that which derives from birth. Every person's birth status is presumed to be honorable, even if it be the status of a beggar. One purpose of genealogies in the ancient world is to make an honor claim. The fact that Jesus is given two different genealogies (one in Luke and another in Matthew) reflects the cultural belief that genealogies serve chiefly to prove one's honorable origins according to the needs of the moment.

Still, people were annoyed by Jesus. Neighbors in his hometown said: "'Is this not the carpenter, the son of Mary and brother of James and Joses and Judas and Simon, and are not his sisters here with us?' And they took offense at him" (Mark 6:3) because Jesus was overstepping his ascribed honor (see Jesus' comment in the very next verse). His neighbors challenged his fundamental claims to honor.

DECEPTION IN THE SERVICE OF HONOR

As Jesus' neighbors demonstrate, a major occupation among Mediterranean people is minding everybody else's business.

Life is very public, and everyone tries to know as much about everyone else in the village as possible. This renders it very difficult to make honor claims.

Because of this cultural tendency to nosiness, people are driven to secrecy and deception as a means of preserving honor. Indeed, even though criticized and repudiated, secrecy and deception are perceived as legitimate strategies for preserving honor. The strategy even follows a process, and it is evident in Jesus' exchange with his disciples in today's reading.

PROCESS OF SECRECY

The process of secrecy involves insiders and outsiders. Basically, an insider (and sometimes his faction) have a secret, which outsiders will try to ferret out. The secrecy process has five stages:

1. **Insider.** The insider has a secret; this carries with it power and security.

2. **Outsider.** Outsiders try to learn the secret through surveillance, espionage, etc.

3. **Insider.** The secret-holder devises security methods, including deception, which includes leaking false information, to preserve the secret.

4. **Outsider.** Nosy people must now evaluate what they have previously suspected or spied out and compare it to the fresh information that has been given to them.

5. **Insider.** The insider may be satisfied with that confusion or may seek to lead the process further.

JESUS AND SECRECY

In today's reading, the secrecy process appears to develop in this fashion:

1. **Insider.** Jesus knows his self-identity, his origins (see Mark 6:3), but as a typical Mediterranean dyadic personality, he needs to know what others think. He asks his disciples what they have heard.

2. **Outsiders.** The crowds think Jesus is John the Baptist, or Elijah, or another ancient prophet come back to life.

3. **Insider.** Jesus asks his followers (other insiders) for their opinion. Peter says: "The Messiah of God." Jesus commands him and the others not to tell anyone. True to the process, Jesus leaves it to the outsiders to weigh all their knowledge and draw a conclusion. The association of Jesus with the Baptist, Elijah, or other prophets, though incorrect, are, in Jesus' mind, honorable attributes. Why disturb these misconceptions?

4. **Outsiders.** The crowds are still left with their three opinions, and if the disciples (insiders) leak the secret, the outsiders will have four opinions to weigh. They must sort all this out.

5. **Insider.** Jesus's full identity and reputation are known to him alone. Others, like the neighbors in his hometown, are still in the dark. They may still try to shame him, but they will never be certain of a good basis for shaming him. His honor remains intact. This is the "payoff" of deception in the service of honor.

Modern believers are understandably troubled by this use of deception as a strategy for maintaining honor. Modern Americans have laws safeguarding truth in advertising and guaranteeing open meetings of governmental agencies. Other agencies assure that weights and measure are honest, and so on, ad infinitum. Lacking these guarantees of honesty and truth, the Mediterranean people whose lives are reflected in the Bible had to rely on oaths or statements such as "Amen, amen" (or "Truly, truly") to assure others that they were not lying. Even this was much misused, else there would be no need for a commandment forbidding the calling of God to witness to a lie ("using the Lord's name in vain").

Thirteenth Sunday in Ordinary Time
Luke 9:51-62

Three key geographical regions of first-century Palestine were Galilee, Samaria, and Judea. By the time of Jesus' ministry, Samaritans and Judeans had experienced seven hundred years of tense and hostile relationships, even while acknowledging Jacob as their common patriarch (see John 4:12).

When Samaritans refused hospitality to Jesus' "advance men" (Luke 9:52-53), his disciples quite typically did not hesitate to wish destruction upon them (v. 54). What prompted this traditional, mutual enmity between Judeans and Samaritans?

ASSYRIAN INVASION, 721 B.C.

Sargon the Assyrian defeated the northern kingdom, Israel, around 721 B.C., deported most of the native population, and resettled aliens in their place in Samaria (2 Kgs 17:24-41). These intermarried with the remaining natives, prompting the Judeans to label the Samaritans an impure people. Judeans would have nothing to do with Samaritans (see John 4:9).

BABYLONIAN EXILE, 587–537 B.C.

When the Judeans returned from their exile in 537 B.C., their antipathy toward the Samaritans prompted an outright rejection of the Samaritan offer to collaborate in rebuilding the Jerusalem Temple (Ezra 4:1-4).

THE SAMARITAN TEMPLE

After the death of Alexander the Great in 323 B.C., a group of Samaritans disenfranchised by the Greek rulers rebuilt Samaria and its ancient city, Shechem. This same group eventually built a Samaritan temple to Yahweh on Mount Gerizim (see John 4).

Hostilities and disagreements about proper worship dot the centuries-long history of relationships between the Judeans and Samaritans.

FIRST-CENTURY EXPERIENCES

In the first century B.C. Pompey rebuilt Samaria, and Herod the Great (the Idumean hated by the Judeans) built a city in Samaria that included a temple to Caesar Augustus. He called the city "Sebaste," the honorific Greek title of Roman emperors. Understandably, the Samaritans in this period enjoyed Roman favor and protection, while the Judeans were less fortunate. Then two events brought their mutual tensions to a peak.

1. During Passover sometime between A.D. 6 and 9, some Samaritans snuck into the Jerusalem Temple and strew bones throughout, disrupting the Passover observance for that year.

2. In A.D. 51 Samaritans in the village of Gema murdered a Judean Passover pilgrim en route to Jerusalem. Judeans retaliated by massacring the entire village and burning it. The Roman governor, Cumanus, avenged the Samaritans by punishing the Judeans, who in their turn persuaded the Syrian governor Qaudratus to punish the Samaritans and banish Cumanus.

These two events constitute the immediate background for understanding Judean hostility to the Samaritans in the New Testament, and Luke's heroic attempt to defuse it.

LUKE'S JESUS AND THE SAMARITANS

While Matthew's Jesus commands his disciples to "enter no town of the Samaritans" (10:5), Luke's Jesus rebukes these same disciples who would call down fire from heaven upon inhospitable Samaritans (Luke 9:55). He rejects this "eye for eye, tooth for tooth" mentality.

Further, Luke creates and inserts a "good" Samaritan into a story whose traditional cultural progression required a Judean layperson as the third character, after the priest and Levite (Luke 10:25-37).

In addition, Luke's Jesus exhibits special sensitivity to the Samaritan leper among the ten cleansed (17:11-19) by omitting the recommendation of "offering the prescribed sacrifice" as in Matthew 8:2. The Samaritan gift would not be welcome in the Jerusalem Temple.

Finally, in Acts 8:5-8, 14-17, Luke adopts a clever strategy to persuade alienated kin–Samaritans and Judeans–to be reconciled. In Luke's story line the Samaritans believed the word preached by the Hellenist Philip but received the Spirit from the Judeans Peter and John.

This artificial separation of the Spirit from baptism is Luke's intentional strategy for stirring Samaritan respect for and loyalty to Jerusalem and Judeans. It also aims at improving understanding between Judeans and Samaritans.

For contemporary American believers, this thumbnail sketch of historical relationships between Judeans and Samaritans and Luke's masterful efforts at reconciliation poses this challenge: should we allow cultural and historical differences to divide us? Is there only one way to serve God? or to love Jesus? or to be Christian?

Who or what can help us appreciate the integral and rightful place in the Christian community of those culturally different from us?

Fourteenth Sunday in Ordinary Time
Luke 10:1-12, 17-20

Two very distinctive Mediterranean ideas strike the Western reader in this passage: hospitality and human power over the spirit world.

HOSPITALITY

In the Mediterranean world hospitality is extended almost exclusively by men and only to strangers. Graciousness extended to relatives or near relatives is called "steadfast love" or "steadfast loving kindness."

In the ancient world, any person who departed from the family village entered a foreign and hostile world. Death was always and everywhere a threat. Such a traveler had to rely on the kindness of a village elder to extend hospitality and temporary protection from those who intended to harm or kill this stranger (see Gen 18:1-16; 19:1-26). Jesus, therefore, utters a cultural truism when he says to the seventy: "I am sending you as lambs into the midst of wolves"–strangers among nonrelatives (Luke 10:3).

HEALING: HOSPITALITY REWARDED

In the peasant world of the Middle East there are no free gifts. Every gift comes with a string attached. A common proverb says: "Don't thank me; you will repay me."

Jesus advises his disciples to be discriminating in accepting hospitality on their journey. If the host reciprocates their greeting of "peace," the disciples should stay there and preach and heal the sick.

On the other hand, if the town insults them by refusing to extend hospitality, they are to go to the town square (a very public place) and publicly return the insult. Both gestures—healing and preaching, and the public insult—bear witness that "the reign of God approaches and is indeed near."

POWER OVER SPIRITS

Our Mediterranean ancestors in the Faith not only recognized a rich and densely populated spirit world, but they also arranged the entire cosmos in a hierarchy as follows: (1) God; (2) gods or sons of God, or archangels; (3) lower non-human persons: angels, spirits, demons; (4) humankind; (5) creatures lower than humankind.

Beings higher on this ladder controlled those beneath them, but sometimes—though very rarely—a lower being could control a higher being. Notice in the New Testament that no one denies the reality of Jesus casting demons out of possessed persons. Rather, they charge that he has no legitimate authorization to use this power (Luke 20:2) or that he has obtained his power from the devil (Luke 11:15).

Jesus, in turn, gave this same power to his disciples. Sometimes it was not effective (Luke 9:40), but in today's story it seems to have been very effective: "Lord, in your name, even the demons submit to us!" (Luke 10:17).

Some literal Western readers of the Bible misunderstand Jesus' description of the power he has shared with his disciples. His statement is arranged in parallelism:

> I have given you authority
> to tread on snakes and scorpions,
> and over all the power of the Enemy [the devil];
> he [the enemy] shall harm you in nothing (Luke 10:19).

Snakes and scorpions were not only potentially harmful realities in the daily life of our Middle-Eastern ancestors, but they were also popular symbols of evil throughout the Old Testament. The serpent is part of the explanation of the origin of "evil" in human life (see Gen 3:1-14; Num 21:6-9; Sir 21:2). The scorpion is a symbol of divine punishment (1 Kgs 12:11, 14) and is already combined with snakes in a similar way in Deuteronomy 8:15. Luke repeats this combination in 11:11-12, where the reference is to the yellow scorpion, which sometimes looks like an egg.

Jesus' statement, therefore, explains what the seventy have accomplished: nothing less than placing under Jesus' own "authority" all aspects of demonic evil: physical, symbolic, and personal.

MODERN REFLECTIONS

Mediterranean notions of hospitality and human power over demons do not translate readily into contemporary Western culture. Americans prefer to restrict hospitality to known and cherished friends and to treat strangers in the accepted American style: with the anonymity of the motel or the rescue mission. Perhaps our multicultural society needs to explore new ways to recognize its "strangers" as the fellow- and sister-citizens they actually are.

Similarly, the eminently *personal* approach to life's problems (e.g., demons) in the Mediterranean world could balance the cold, impersonal, scientifically objective approach to life in the West.

Fifteenth Sunday in Ordinary Time
Luke 10:25-37

QUESTIONS AND HONOR

In the Mediterranean world questions are rarely perceived as requests for information. They are almost always viewed with suspicion as a challenge to personal honor. The hope is that the person who is asked a question will not know the answer and be shamed by ignorance. Lest the reader miss the point, Luke explicitly states that the lawyer's intent was to "test" Jesus.

Here and throughout the Gospel, Jesus responds in a consistent way. He always insults his questioner. Jesus asks a lawyer, a specialist in the Torah (the *written* word of God): "How do you *read?*"

The lawyer answers his own question correctly by quoting Deuteronomy 6:4-5 and Leviticus 19:18, thereby revealing that he knew the answer all along. His question was not simply a test of Jesus, it was a lie. He pretended to be ignorant though he wasn't. Instead of shaming Jesus, the lawyer shames himself, and Jesus emerges—once again—the honorable victor in this contest.

The lawyer has one more chance to "save face" (or as most translations render it, "justify himself"). He asks Jesus another question: "Who is my neighbor?" Jesus recognizes this question as yet another lie, because the context of Leviticus 19:18, which the lawyer just quoted correctly, explicitly notes that neighbor is "your kin," "your people."

The lawyer has now told two lies: one to cause trouble for Jesus and another to salvage his own sinking reputation. Jesus' masterfully crafted parable lays the final lash of shame on the humbled back of this arrogant lawyer.

THE GOOD SAMARITAN

In this seven-scene parable, the Samaritan stands at the center:

1. The robbers strip and leave their victim half dead (v. 30). Now, no one can identify the victim's ethnicity by his garments or his accent, two very common ways of identifying a stranger in antiquity. Helping him carries a risk.

2. The priest, riding a donkey in accord with his elite status, notices the victim and ponders. If the victim is dead or is a non-Judean, the priest would be defiled by touching him and have to return to Jerusalem for purification. Those who just saw him gloriously fulfilling his priestly role would now see him returning in shame for purification. The risk is too great. Recalling Sirach 12:1-7, the priest rides on (v. 31).

3. The Levite may have come even closer to examine the victim (v. 32). Even though the road is not straight, the Levite very likely saw the priest's response to the victim from afar. If the priest did not give first aid, why should the Levite? That would be a challenge to the priest, an insult. Moreover, if this victim is one of those who live in Shechem (i.e., a Samaritan), Sirach 50:25-26 reports what God thinks of such. The Levite, too, passes on.

4. The Samaritan is a shocking third character in this story. Listeners would have expected "a Judean layperson." But this hated enemy is the first to feel compassion (v. 33)! The Hebrew word, related to womb, describes an inner gut-feeling.

5. He offers the first aid (wine, oil, and bandages), which the Levite could have done but neglected to do (v. 34). The Samaritan's risk is that this victim might hate him upon regaining consciousness. Samaritan wine and oil were con-

sidered impure and would have made the (very likely) Judean victim impure too! In a certain sense, the Samaritan in this story line will be "damned if he does, and damned if he doesn't."

6. The Samaritan then does what the priest might have done but didn't: he places the victim on his animal, takes him to an inn, and continues to care for him (v. 34)

7. Finally, the Samaritan, in contrast to the robbers, promises to return and pay any additional expenses (v. 35). This is perhaps the most foolish part of this story. If the victim should die, his family, who will not be able to find the robbers, may kill his benefactor instead. Or if the victim survives, he may rage at this Samaritan for making him impure with Samaritan wine and oil. It is impossible to underestimate the importance of purity, that is, the determination to "be holy as the Lord is holy" (Lev 11:44 and elsewhere).

The thrust of the parable is not lost on the lawyer. His face is still red with shame from Jesus' earlier insult. Now Jesus thrusts the final shaming question: "Which of the three *became a neighbor* to the victim?"

The astute lawyer immediately recognizes this new, impending shame. The lawyer's question was: "Who is my neighbor?" Jesus' question is: "To whom must you become a neighbor?" The lawyer realizes that one must become a neighbor to anyone and everyone in need. One must reach out with compassion to all people, even to one's enemies.

Too often this parable has been read as a pleasant moral lesson of kindness and neighborliness. Fleshing out all the characters in their Mediterranean cultural characteristics gives the parable a fresh look. A hated outsider extends compassionate love to his enemy. What a masterful attack on communal prejudice!

Sixteenth Sunday in Ordinary Time
Luke 10:38-42

In the recently published *Women's Bible Commentary* (Westminster/John Knox), University of Detroit Mercy Professor Jane Schaberg observes that commentaries on this story reveal that "there is no agreement about its basic meaning." Interpretations generally focus on the contrast between the two sisters and their activities. Traditionally they have been said to represent the active and contemplative life, justification by faith and justification by works, Judaism and Christianity, conflicting women's careers and priorities, and so on.

Contemporary feminist interpreters propose that Jesus here champions a woman's right to theological education and ministry on par with men. Elisabeth Schüssler Fiorenza believes Luke is prescribing women's roles in eucharistic table service for the Church of that time and not reporting something that was common then or earlier.

These highly imaginative interpretations often seem to be relevant to concerns contemporary with the interpreter rather than the evangelist. Scholars still wonder whether these interpretations are historically or culturally plausible.

Closer reflection on the Mediterranean cultural elements in this story raise yet another plausible interpretation.

CULTURAL ELEMENTS

The 1986 revision of the *New American Bible* New Testament reports that Martha welcomes Jesus but omits the phrase "to her home." This is based on ancient Greek manuscripts, which omit this phrase.

In some parts of the Mediterranean world, the oldest girl generally inherits the mother's home (women own it) and receives the name of her grandmother. The firstborn son takes on the trade of his father and the name of his grandfather.

In 10:32, Luke refers to Martha's home; but earlier, in 4:38, Jesus enters *Simon's* house, while Mark identifies it as Simon and Andrew's house. The references seem not to identify the owner of the home so much as those who are playing key roles in the story. Here, that would be Martha.

More stunning in the story is the fact that Jesus seems to be alone in a home with two women who are not his relatives! Given the difficulty Jesus—or anyone—has in being alone in this culture (see 5:42), it is plausible to think that at least some of his disciples have accompanied him. Moreover, Mediterranean homes are the dwellings of large extended families, including fictive kin.

Though not explicitly mentioned here, it is plausible that the women's brother, Lazarus, is also present (see John 11). He would behave very shamefully as a brother if he did not chaperon his sisters in the presence or an unrelated male. Moreover, in this situation, Lazarus appears to be the key male in the lives of his unmarried and/or widowed sisters. He is their guardian, their social security. His death would put the sisters into the same predicament as the widow of Nain (Luke 7:11-17, see Tenth Sunday in Ordinary Time).

Perhaps the most stunning cultural element in the story is that Jesus appears to be teaching a woman. First of all, someone is out of place. In the gender-based division of space in this culture, it is very likely Mary who is sitting with Jesus in an area reserved for men (whether dining area or "living-room" area). Second, even though Jesus may be breaking cultural rules by teaching Mary, she appears to be passive listener, as the feminist interpreters point out. She never is reported to teach in her turn or take up a ministry later.

Third, since Jesus interacts with Mary here and in John 11, Malina suggests that Martha might have been the younger sister.

FRESH INTERPRETATION

In the Mediterranean cultural perspective on human activity men are expected to be spontaneous, to react to the challenge, opportunity, or invitation of the moment (see Luke 7:31-35). Women are expected to work, achieve, to be involved in purposeful activity. When men are healed in Luke, they respond spontaneously and run out to spread the word. When Simon's mother-in-law is healed, her first response is the measured activity of serving a meal. Jesus' positive judgment that "Mary has chosen the good part" and his gentle reminder to Martha for being "worried and distracted about many things" fits into Jesus' customary, counter-structural positions. He frequently takes his culture's second-choice options for either gender, in this case "spontaneous" behavior among women, and urges it as a good alternative to the first choice ("achievement"). For men, he regularly urges that they who hold spontaneity as their primary activity look instead to methodical and thoughtful "doing" of the will of God, "keeping" the commandments, and so on.

According to Luke's Jesus, when there is a choice between extending steadfast loving kindness (Martha) and listening to the word of God (Mary), the latter is preferable.

Seventeenth Sunday in Ordinary Time
Luke 11:1-13

In general, prayer is a form of communication with someone who is considered to be in charge of life. For most believers, God is in charge of life and everything. Americans, who take pride in their scientific abilities and achievements, have gradually reduced the areas of life of which God is in charge. Only in extreme cases do Americans turns to God regarding needs in the economy, health, space conquest, and so on. This is one reason why American believers sometimes find it difficult to pray.

PRAYER AND PATRONAGE

In the Mediterranean world of our ancestors in the Faith, peasants—constituting about 90 percent of the population—realized only too well that they were not in charge of anything. Nature determined their weather and climate. The landowners determined what they might plant and how much they might keep. Rome determined the taxes they should pay—in crops, not in cash! What could a peasant do?

Above all, the peasant could pray, that is, communicate with anyone—including God—who was controlling one or another part of life and hope to obtain benefits from that person. In other words, prayer is a form of communication intended to influence the decision of a patron, someone who looks upon and treats a client, the one praying, *as if* that one were a family member. This is what the disciples ask Jesus to share with them. "Teach us how you communicate with and have an influence upon God."

THE LORD'S PRAYER

Jesus encourages the disciples to address God as "Father," just as he does (see 10:21; 22:42). In other words, Jesus says: "Consider God as a Father, as one who is as near as and behaves just like a father toward his children." In the Middle East this kind of relationship is called "patronage," and someone who behaves like a father to people who are not his children is a "patron."

The patron can get things for clients that the client could not obtain by personal ability, or on better terms than the client could manage by personal ability. This is the appropriate context for interpreting the five petitions of Luke's version of the Lord's Prayer.

Praise of the Father/patron. The first two petitions praise God as children would praise a father. These first two petitions concern things no human could achieve but that God can easily achieve with divine power. "To hallow one's name" is to "be in truth who you really are": Father, patron, truly in charge of life. "Your kingdom come" urges God to achieve and establish kingly dominion once-and-for-always, definitively, over all of life.

Three human needs. The plurals in these petitions give the prayer a communal rather than an individual dimension. This accords with the Mediterranean cultural preference for groups over individuals. Having praised God, the community can now ask for daily sustenance, forgiveness of sins, and preservation from temptation to apostasy. Jesus encourages petitioners to present these petitions with confidence that they will be granted. Whence this confidence?

GOD'S HONOR

In the following parable, wherein a friend asks a friend for help in hosting unexpected visitors, the word most often translated "persistence" should be translated "shamelessness."

Recall the Mediterranean obligation of extending a safe sojourn to strangers passing through a village (Genesis 19). Caught unprepared, one such host begs a friend for bread, the staple of every meal, that he might fulfill the village obligation of extending hospitality.

The friend gives excuses until the petitioner threatens to expose his "shameless" behavior to the entire village in the morning. The man who declined to share his bread jeopardized his honorable status. Honor is more important than sleep, and that thought alone was sufficient to rouse the man from a comfortable bed and share the bread he had.

God is like the man in bed. He is sensitive about his honor (see Ezek 36:16-28) and will not risk having his clients expose divine shamelessness for refusing to take care of them as a good father or patron should.

This is how people think about God in Mediterranean culture. What is the American technique for influencing God?

Eighteenth Sunday in Ordinary Time
Luke 12:13-21

Bible readers are very familiar with stories of enmity between brothers in ancient Mediterranean families: Jacob and Esau (Genesis 27); Joseph and his eleven brothers (Genesis 37). Inheritance was often a key cause of the enmity.

The brothers praised in Psalm 133:1 for living together in unity illustrate the situation where a father died and did not specify a division of the inheritance. According to Roman law, a division of inheritance was required only if *both* parties wanted it. Judaic law allowed the division on the petition of a single son (see Luke 15:12), but it was shameful because it effectively expressed the wish that the father were already dead.

JESUS THE MEDIATOR

In today's story Jesus is invited to be a mediator, a very difficult but highly honorable role in this culture. Conflicts can easily escalate to blood feuds that no one wants. The key role of the mediator is to head off the blood feuds. The role is honored and advocated in the Matthean Beatitudes (5:9): "Truly worthy of esteem, truly honorable are the *peacemakers*, for they will be considered God-like."

Ideally the mediator is a kinsperson at least five links removed from the disputing parties. Above all, the mediator should be a person who, because of personality, status, respect, wealth, influence, or other characteristics, can create in the litigants a willingness to conform with his decision.

Jesus responds to the honorable invitation in two ways. First, he adopts the customary role of cultural humility. Paying and receiving compliments is dangerous in this culture. Jesus protects himself against envy and the evil eye by his feigned humility: "Friend, who set me to be judge or arbitrator over you?"

Second, Jesus gives the real reason for his refusal. He suspected he was being drawn into a conflict driven by greed.

INHERITANCE AND GREED

In ancient Mediterranean society the prevailing peasant outlook believed that "there was no more where this came from." Everything–health, wealth, honor–existed in a limited supply that had already been distributed. This amount was sufficient for each person. Anyone who experienced an increase, even if unintentional, was viewed as a thief. Someone else surely has lost. Anyone who intentionally wanted and strove to obtain more was greedy.

Ancient writers confirm these impressions. Aristotle noted: "The amount of such property sufficient in itself for a good life is not unlimited" (*Politics* III, 9, 1256b). Clement of Alexandria observed: "No person is destitute when it comes to the necessities of life, nor is any person overlooked" (*Paidagogos*, II, 14, 5). St. Jerome asserted: "Every rich person is a thief or the heir of a thief" (*On Jeremiah*, II, V, 2).

THE PARABLE AND GREED

In Jesus' parable about the man with the bumper crop, God is not pleased with his plan to "save for the future" in bigger barns. God calls this man a fool! The man deserves God's judgment. The man is clearly a landowner, a minuscule minority in Jesus' world. He appears to live on his land and share in the work of the land. When he realizes the magnitude of his crops, he plans to tear down his barns and build bigger ones.

But his "future planning" is condemned by God and even by the words of the fool himself. "You have ample goods laid up for many years," said the fool. "Relax, eat, drink, and be merry" (v. 19). He stores for future lean years, but not simply for his own pleasure. When the village smallholders have to come to him and borrow grain, he will charge an exorbitant price in hopes of confiscating even more land for himself.

What should the fool have done? The same anyone else in that position should have done: distribute the surplus to others, immediately. The lucky landowner was in a good position to become a "patron," to select even more clients, or simply to be beneficent. He might have done what Jesus praised the shrewd steward for doing (Luke 16:1-9): using surplus wealth as a means to gain friends so that when the wealth is gone, the friends will remain and repay the kindnesses, as this culture expects.

Our ancestors never fail to challenge us.

Nineteenth Sunday
in Ordinary Time
Luke 12:32-48

More than thirty years ago the Pontifical Biblical Commission instructed readers of the synoptic Gospels to pay careful attention to the three stages of tradition in which Jesus' teachings have been handed on: stage one—Jesus himself; stage two—the apostles' preaching; stage three—the evangelists, who composed their Gospels more than forty years after Jesus died. In 1993 the same commission published a document entitled "The Interpretation of the Bible in the Church," in which it praised the insights from cultural anthropology that can shed so much fresh light on the Bible and make the characters and story lines culturally plausible.

These "Sunday by Sunday" reflections attempt to describe the most plausible Mediterranean historical and cultural scenario for the Gospels at any of the levels. The scenario for today's selection helps a reader to see at least two of them rather clearly.

MEDITERRANEAN TIME

Readers need an appropriate "time" scenario to read these verses. While Americans are normally future oriented, peasants are too deeply mired in present concerns such as "daily bread" to think about the future at all. Mediterranean culture is primarily focused on the present, albeit a wide present including tomorrow and yesterday.

Yet verses 35 to 48 clearly have a future thrust. With each generation of believers, the original statement recedes more and more into the past and makes the future seem increasingly distant from the gospel point of view.

The question, therefore, is: Does this future thrust derive from Jesus or from Luke or both? And how far into the future does each one see?

JESUS AND TIME

In the Gospels Jesus often shows himself to be counter-structural in his culture. Where the culture holds one value orientation, Jesus proposes an alternative. Peasants were intensely oriented to the present moment; elites (e.g., the Sadducees) and scholars of the tradition (e.g., the scribes) were primarily oriented to the past. Hardly anyone was oriented toward the future.

The "future" thrust of these verses, which call for watchfulness and fidelity, contrasts strongly with the typical peasant's spontaneous response to the present moment. When the cat's away, the mice will play. When the master is gone, the servant who feels so inspired will beat other slaves, eat, drink, and get drunk (v. 45).

In his typical counter-structural stance, Jesus urges at least a little concern for the future, a rather proximate future. In his parables he speaks of the unpredictable but sure return of the master. He also says: "The Son of Man is coming at an unexpected hour." More about this Son of Man later.

LUKE AND TIME

Writing his Gospel approximately fifty to fifty-five years after the death and resurrection of Jesus, Luke, like his readers, is all too familiar with a common lament. The risen Jesus was expected to return again, but his return is delayed now for some fifty years. Some are dying, others are frustrated, and still others begin to throw care to the winds.

Luke, therefore, calls for continued vigilance and fidelity: "Have your belt cinched tight (freeing the feet for swift movement) and your lamps lit" (v. 35), for "the Son of Man is coming at an unexpected hour" (v. 40).

THE "COMING" SON OF MAN

This phrase appears chiefly on the lips of Jesus in the Gospels as a self-identification; it can often be translated as "I." The majority of these "Son of Man" occurrences in Luke refer to Jesus' ministry (5:24; 6:5, 22; 7:34; 9:56, 58; 11:30; 12:10) or his suffering (9:22, 26, 44). But from this point in Luke (12) forward, references to the Son of Man definitely describe a "future judge" (17:22, 24, 26, 30; 18:89; 21:27, 36; 22:69).

Many scholars believe these "judge" references were created and placed on the lips of Jesus by the early believers as they grew impatient awaiting his imminent return while struggling with the cruel injustices of everyday life. (Notice the cruelty of the unfaithful servant and the violent punishment meted out to such in verses 45–48, a very plausible Mediterranean cultural scenario for Jesus and Luke's readers.)

At some time, the faithful and vigilant believers reasoned, "they [the wicked] will get theirs!" Present-oriented peasants could find consolation in this kind of thinking, and for them a rewarding future was more appealing than the frustrating present.

Americans are quite definitely and primarily future-oriented, and frequently neglect the present. American believers could benefit by imitating the present-orientation of their ancestors in the Faith. This is the kind of balance that Jesus sought in his own culture.

Twentieth Sunday
in Ordinary Time
Luke 12:49-53

SALT AND FIRES

In the Aramaic language that Jesus spoke the word translated as "earth" can also—and in this passage, culturally more plausibly—be translated as "earth-oven."

The "earth-oven," the common stove in Mediterranean villages, was made of mud or clay. The fuel it burned was camel-dung patties, dried and salted so that they would burn better. Salt has mysterious power. The block of salt on the floor of the earth-oven kept the fire going just as much as the salt crystals in the dung patties. Eventually a block of salt in the earth-oven loses its catalytic ability and must be thrown out (Matt 5:13). Salt that can no longer burn the fuel or prepare the fuel is useless (Luke 14:34-35).

SALTY OR FIERY PEOPLE

Jesus came to light the oven (Luke 12:49), that is, Jesus presents himself as a catalyst. He causes fires to break out, arguments to erupt, families to quarrel and become divided in their opinion of him. He urges his disciples likewise to be catalytic and to do the same thing he does (Matt 5:13; Mark 9:49).

How do these notions fit into Luke's Gospel of peace? How does this culturally very plausible idea of Jesus the fire-starter square with Luke's infancy narrative, in which Jesus is expected to bring peace (1:79; 2:14, 29)?

PEACE

One clue is found in the Middle-Eastern concept of peace. The Hebrew word, *shalom,* has at least eight distinctively different meanings. But it never means well-ordered silence, stillness, everything in its orderly place, or other such favorite Western scenarios.

The Middle East is noisy, loud, active, spontaneous. The cultural scenario for one Middle-Eastern concept of peace is children yelling and screaming, adults shouting or quarreling, people singing, and everything in delightful disarray.

Middle-Eastern peace even includes normal family rivalries. Remember the petitioner who greedily asked Jesus to persuade his brother to share the inheritance (see Luke 12:13; Deut 21:17)? Recall how Rebekah advised her son, Jacob, to dupe his father, Isaac, into giving him the inheritance (Genesis 27)? Reflect upon the intrigues of David's family (1–2 Samuel). And what Westerner can fail to be stunned at the "normal" palace politics that made Solomon king (1 Kings 1–2).

Even fictive family groups engaged in normal competition. What do you think about the brothers, James and John, seeking the highest places of honor in Jesus' retinue of twelve (Mark 10:35), or all twelve arguing at the Last Supper about who is the greatest (Luke 22:24)?

JESUS THE "DIVISIVE CATALYST"

Jesus' assertion that he will cause division in families is obviously something above and beyond the normal Mediterranean family and group shenanigans noted above. It is far more serious.

The sharp delineation of social hierarchy that characterized antiquity was rigidly observed by all. No one dared step out of the inherited or assigned place. To do so would be to risk death. One move in this deadly direction would be to socialize with people outside of one's social position. Contemporaries of Jesus who liked him and decided to follow him would also have to join his fictive family group. "My mother and brothers," that is, my new, fictive relatives, said Jesus, "are those who hear the word of God and do it!" (Luke 8:21).

To separate oneself from one's family or clan is literally a matter of life and death. Elites, (including the "greedy [rich]" whom Luke so often includes in his Gospel), would lose everything, all their wealth, power, and influence, by associating with the wrong kind of people or joining the wrong kinds of groups.

Joining Jesus' group also jeopardized one's relations with the very large kinship network formed by marriage, a network far larger than the biological family. This is where the in-laws and other such family members enter the picture (Luke 12:52-53).

By demonstrating how to be catalysts for the fire in the earth-oven and summoning us to be and do the same, Jesus challenges American believers. Our culture takes pride in its faith in God, but we believe religion and politics should not mix. Clergy may pray before legislative sessions and bless conflicts, but criticism and protest are not welcome.

Who among us is salt of the earth?

Twenty-First Sunday in Ordinary Time
Luke 13:22-30

The Mishnah (ca. A.D. 200), a collection of rabbinic laws as applied to detailed aspects of Jewish daily life, reflects a common belief among Palestinian Judeans of Jesus' day that "all Israelites have a share in the world to come" (*Sanhedrin* 10:1). But the Pharisees reflected a Judean tradition that believed that only a "remnant" would be saved. "This age the Most High has made for many, but the age to come for few" (4 Ezra 8:1). It is in this context that Jesus' Judean listeners wanted to know how many Judeans would have a share in the kingdom that he was preaching.

Instead of giving a direct answer to the question (which is only God's business anyway), Jesus highlights the need for strenuous effort to overcome an anticipated traffic jam at the narrow door. Many unworthy people will try to squeeze in.

Here is the scenario for the reflection that follows. The master of the house is Jesus himself. Jesus' contemporaries, who know him well, have listened to his teaching, and even supped with him, now make a bold claim to deserve entry to the banquet. Jesus not only denies knowing them but calls them "evildoers" and chases them away. In fact, he locks them out.

"INSIDERS" AND "OUTSIDERS"

Our group-oriented ancestors in the Faith put their primary and greatest faith in the family. This was the core of the "inside"; everyone else was "outside." At a higher level, the chosen people of God were the "insiders," while all others were outsiders.

The normal way to become an "insider" is to be born into the family or group. But all societies recognize other ways of becoming an "insider." One general method is to share the same substance that a natural-born child would share with the parents. Thus unrelated children who share the same wet nurse become kin to each other and may not marry each other. Or, two unrelated individuals who share blood become "blood relatives." Societies often select a common bodily substance (blood, saliva, semen, or milk), which when commingled establishes a relationship of kinship between two people.

TABLE FELLOWSHIP

A second way of becoming "related," or becoming "an insider," is by the exchange of food through commensality, or eating together. Friendships are sealed and strangers are integrated into the community by sharing a common meal, even when the ritual aspects of this act of eating together are not explicit.

This understanding of table fellowship lies at the heart of Paul's argument in Galatians 1–2. Peter the Judean used to eat with Gentile converts (non-Judeans) and with this ritual action clearly proclaimed that Judean and non-Judean believers in Jesus were kin. When some Judean believers scolded Peter for eating with believers in Jesus who had not also been circumcised (that is, who had not become Judeans first before becoming messianists), Peter stopped eating with the non-Judean believers. Paul was livid. Peter's withdrawal from table fellowship with non-Judean believers in Jesus amounted to saying that these non-Judeans were not really related or part of the same family as Judean believers in Jesus.

EATING WITH JESUS

Jesus' contemporaries in Luke 13 are claiming the same thing. "By eating with us, Jesus, you have made us kin with you. We are your fictive relatives. Why now are you excluding us from fellowship?" Jesus' answer has already been given earlier in this same chapter (Luke 13:2 and 5): "Unless you repent, you will all perish. . . ." It is not enough to have shared a meal with Jesus. A radical change of life is also necessary to establish a kinship relationship with him.

Jesus' contemporaries remind him: "You taught in our streets." Jesus' harsh reply to them insinuates: "Yes, but all you did was listen. You did not take my teaching to heart and reform your lives. You think superficial acquaintance with me and my teachings suffices." Jesus offers a prophetic warning to believers of all times. Only those will join him at the heavenly banquet who seek to understand him and his message, who seek to learn "the honest truth about Jesus" (Vatican II, Dogmatic Constitution on Divine Revelation, 19).

Twenty-Second Sunday in Ordinary Time
Luke 14:1, 7-14

In Jesus' Mediterranean world meals were very powerful means of communication. Above all, meals affirmed and gave legitimacy to a person's role and status in a given community. For this reason, most meals in antiquity were attended by people of the same social rank. The fact that the ruler of the Pharisees invited Jesus to dine at his house indicates that the Pharisees accepted Jesus as a social equal.

HOSTILITY

The host and his guests were "watching" Jesus closely. The word used here and elsewhere in Luke (6:7; 20:20) implies "hostile observation." They hope to catch him in a short-coming of some sort. The apparently "honorable" invitation is actually hypocritical.

Behavior at these meals is very important. Everyone watches whether one washes (11:38); who eats what, when, and where (6:4); what is done or omitted at table (7:38, 40, 44, 49); who is invited (14:12-14); where people sit (14:7-11); with whom one eats (15:2); and in what order persons of different rank come to the table (17:7-8).

Jesus responds to this hostile observation by telling them a parable. A parable always means something the same and something other. The storyteller challenges the listeners to identify the "other."

TRUE HONOR

This challenge is not lost on the guests, lawyers and Pharisees invited along with Jesus by the host, a leader of the Pharisees. Matthew informs his readers that the Pharisees "love to have the place of honor at banquets" (23:6). Seeing the guests jockey for more honorable seats at this table, Jesus tells his parable.

As it stands, Jesus' parable echoes familiar biblical teaching. Proverbs 25:6-7 and Sirach 3:17-20 prescribe similar and quite expected cultural humility. The centrality of honor in this culture teaches natives to stay always a step behind their rightful status. This clearly demonstrates that one is not at all trying to appear or to be better than another person.

Staying a step behind allows a person to be honored by the host who will invite one to take a higher and more noble position at the banquet.

The guests at this banquet know these cultural rules, but true to type (as described by Matthew), the Pharisees nonetheless prefer to seek their honorable positions.

It is Jesus' conclusion that is shocking. The passive voice ("will be humbled" and "will be exalted," v. 11; see also Luke 18:14) in the Bible ordinarily means God is the one who performs these actions. With this grammatical construction, Jesus reminds his honor-conscious friends at table that God determines authentic honorable status. The opinions of human beings, especially friends and cronies, is unreliable.

TRUE HONOR AGAIN

Accepting an invitation to dinner in the ancient Mediterranean world obligated a guest to return the favor. It was not uncommon for guests to decline the invitation, especially if they realized that returning the favor was more than they could or cared to handle (see Luke 14:15-24).

Crass as this may seem to modern Western believers, this practice of reciprocity was a key factor in the economic life of equals in Jesus' day. I do you a favor; you do me a favor—endlessly. This basic rule of behavior guided every host in drawing up the guest list.

Jesus' advice to his host (v. 12) is not only rude and insulting but also shocking. It is extremely bad manners for a guest to tell a host how to be a host!

Moreover, inviting people who cannot return the favor is viewed as cultural suicide. Such guests—the poor, crippled, lame, and blind (v. 13)—are clearly people of a lower social status than the host. To associate with such is to dishonor one's own status. One's social equals will then shun future invitations, and a host of means will be socially ruined.

Jesus, however, paints another picture of "true" honor. It is not human judgment, the return invitation, that determines honor. God determines true honor, and at the resurrection of the righteous, God personally will reward and honor the host who has been gracious to those unable to return an invitation.

This statement surely stung the Pharisees, who believed in the resurrection (Acts 23:6). Having set a trap for Jesus, they are themselves trapped by Jesus, whose teachings truly turn the world upside-down (see Acts 17:6).

Twenty-Third Sunday in Ordinary Time
Luke 14:25-33

On the face of it, Jesus seems to propose three devastating and inhuman requirements for becoming his disciple: hate one's family (v. 25); carry the cross (v. 26); give up all possessions (v. 33)—even though "half" sufficed for Zacchaeus in 19:8). As usual, the literary context and a culturally appropriate reading scenario help us "foreigners" to better understand our strange-sounding ancestors in the faith.

LITERARY CONTEXT

Jesus has been invited for a meal at the home of a leading Pharisee (Luke 24:1). The cultural world of Jesus required that people—especially the elite—"eat with their own kind, within their own class." The fact that Jesus is often a guest of Pharisees has led some scholars to suggest that Jesus himself was a Pharisee. Whatever the case, he never failed to challenge their beliefs and practices in the interest of offering better alternatives.

CULTURAL BACKGROUND

The purpose of meals in the Middle East was to cement social relationships. Kin and friends were and continue to be the basis of economic survival in this world, where economics was deeply embedded in kinship and politics. You could always count on your family and friends to look after you. The crippled man who admitted having "no one" (family or friends) to put him into the stirred waters (John 5) is a pitiful and tragic Mediterranean character.

True honor. Jesus begins his table remarks with a cultural truism. He reminds his eating partners that true honor is bestowed by others, in this case, the host (vv. 7–11). Choosing to sit where one does not belong at a banquet is shameful. Even so, Jesus' comments likely did not faze the pushy and conceited guests.

The Guest List. Next (vv. 12–14) Jesus turns the cultural world completely upside down by urging that hosts should invite guests who could *not* reciprocate: "the poor, crippled, blind, and lame" (v. 21). If one took this seriously, a host—quite obviously a person with means, that is, a home and the wherewithal to feed others—would soon run out of means. Who would then look after him?

HATING ONE'S FAMILY

It is this Middle-Eastern understanding of "meals" that helps a "foreigner" to understand Jesus' comments on discipleship in today's reading. A follower of Jesus who ceased "networking" by means of meals would jeopardize a family's very existence. The disciple must then choose between allegiance to the family and allegiance to Jesus. Choosing Jesus is thus equivalent to letting one's family go, "hating" the family. Hate is more suitably translated "prefer," that is, one who "hates" family actually prefers another group to the family.

Recall the tight-knit nature of the Middle-Eastern family. The ideal marriage partner is a first cousin. Sons, married and single, remain with the father. Everyone "controls" one another. Life in these circumstances can be very stifling, very suffocating. Following Jesus and joining a new, fictive family would be very liberating and exhilarating.

CARRYING THE CROSS

There is, of course, a price to pay for such freedom. In the Middle East, the main rule of behavior is: family first! A disciple who deliberately cuts ties with family and social network will lose the ordinary means of making a living. This is the "economic cross" the disciple has chosen to carry. True, by joining a new, fictive family consisting of other disciples of Jesus, a "family-hating" person presumably has a new source of livelihood.

No longer able to make claims to a livelihood based on blood ties and advantageous social network, members of this new fictive family have to rely on "hospitality," which in the Middle East is extended exclusively by strangers to strangers (see Luke 9:4-5; 10:3-12). This risk-filled option is quite a cross to carry.

GIVE UP ALL POSSESSIONS

Clearly, a disciple who has accepted these challenging exhortations will effectively have given up everything. Therefore, a would-be disciple must seriously calculate the costs. Two brief parables (about construction and waging war) drive this point home. Anyone who weakens and abandons this determination will become the butt of ridicule and shame. A disciple must remain firmly committed. The behavior Jesus proposes is liberating and heroic but costly. Jesus' attitude toward family values give his followers much to think about. Contemporary believers are challenged to reflect upon the meaning of "family values" in the ancient Mediterranean world and whether it is possible to import them into other contemporary cultures.

Twenty-Fourth Sunday
in Ordinary Time
Luke 15:1-32

A rabbinic tradition cautions: "Let not a person associate with sinners even to bring them near to the Torah" (*Mekilta* 57b on Exod 18:1). Feeding sinners is praiseworthy; eating with them is forbidden. "Hosting" or "welcoming" sinners, as Jesus does here (15:2), makes the Pharisees furious.

JESUS, MASTER OF INSULT

Jesus routinely deals with opponents by insulting them plainly and directly. The central characters of the twin parables are deeply offensive to the Pharisees.

Shepherds. For all their rich symbolism in Scripture, shepherds were considered by the Pharisees as unclean, members of a despised and forbidden profession. Jesus sarcastically asks the Pharisees, "Which *one of you*, having a hundred sheep and losing one . . . ?"

Women. It would have been an unpardonable insult if Jesus had said to this group of oriental men: "Which *woman* of you . . . ?" so he abbreviates and generalizes his question: "Which woman losing a coin . . . ?"

In both stories something of great value is lost: one, of a hundred sheep, the other, of ten coins. The sheep is lost in the wilderness; the coin is lost in a home. The sheep must be restored to the community, for it is a communal loss. A family might have forty sheep at most. One hundred sheep clearly belong to more than one family. The coin is easily rejoined to the woman's jewelry, of which it is a part.

The point of each story is that a diligent search will find the treasured loss and bring enormous joy. Pharisees should rejoice rather than grumble over Jesus' search for and reconciliation of lost sinners.

THE TWO LOST SONS

Jesus draws the Pharisees even closer with another double parable featuring a younger son (vv. 11–24) and an older son (25–32, see also Fourth Sunday of Lent, above).

Sin. The younger son's request is equivalent to wishing his father were dead. By refusing to reconcile the younger son with father, the older son is equally remiss.

Repentance. Having squandered the inheritance, being reduced to tending unclean animals, and beginning to starve, the younger son "came to himself," that is, "began to repent." He acknowledged that by losing the inheritance he lost the means for taking care of his father in old age. Opting to become a hired servant would preserve his independence and enable him to build up the funds he lost and repay his father. Repentance will bring reconciliation with his father, but probably not with his brother or with the village.

Grace. The father's behavior toward his returning son are dramatic deeds calculated to protect the boy from the anticipated hostility of the village. He runs the village gauntlet to meet the boy, wraps him in a protective hug, and kisses him again and again in a sign of reconciliation and forgiveness.

Joy. Killing a calf rather than a goat or sheep means the entire community is invited to share in the joy. There is food enough here for more than a hundred people. The banquet is intended to reconcile the boy with the entire community.

Sonship. The father confirms the reestablished relationship: "This son of mine was dead and is alive again; was lost and is found." This is more than the boy dreamed of. The elder son, too, is lost. He refuses to join in the feasting. Instead, he publicly humiliates his father by arguing with him in the presence of the entire village. He addresses his father with no title. He repudiates his sonship ("I have *slaved* for you!"). Amid his insults, the elder son insists, "I have never disobeyed you." He accuses the father of favoritism ("him a calf; me not even a goat"). He slanders his brother by introducing into the story an unfounded charge of cavorting with harlots.

How does the father respond? Once again he treats an offending son with love tendered in humiliation. The father addresses the boy with a title, "Son," and assures him that his share of inheritance is intact. In return for arrogance, the father offers compassion.

The two sons in this parable are essentially the same and equally offensive. They differ only in their response to unexpected and undeserved love demonstrated by their humiliated father. Like these sons, all who hear this story must decide how they should respond to forgiving love.

Twenty-Fifth Sunday in Ordinary Time
Luke 16:1-13

This parable invariably troubles the capitalistic convictions of American believers. Why would the defrauded master in Jesus' parable "commend his dishonest steward?" What lesson did Jesus intend to teach with this disturbing parable?

ANCIENT ECONOMICS

In the preindustrial world of Jesus, agriculture was the heart of the economy. Modern contrasts such as "rich" and "poor," "urban" and "rural," "industrial" and "agricultural" are irrelevant to this time. The chief issues were who controlled the land and the agricultural production, and who had the power to extract the surplus.

The landowner (16:1) has a steward who manages the agricultural production of his property. The debtors owe the master produce: olive oil and wheat. Money in peasant economies is neither the only nor the predominant medium of exchange.

The Mishnah (postbiblical tradition in Judaic literature) identifies three kinds of renters: some pay a percentage of the crop; some pay a fixed amount of the produce; some pay rent in money. The debtors here seem to be in the second category. A rough modern approximation of their fixed rent is 900 gallons of oil and 150 bushels of wheat. The amount of the debt forgiven by the steward, though different in terms of percentage, nevertheless approximates five hundred denarii.

THE STEWARD'S GENIUS

A steward, or estate manager, was entitled to a commission or fee on each transaction, which itself was recorded, principal and interest, in a public contract. There is no evidence that a steward could extract a fee as high as 50 percent. Peasants would have immediately informed the landowner or would have rioted if a landowner were in collusion with such extortion.

The Mishnah also decrees that an agent should pay for any losses he caused his employer. This steward is extremely fortunate. He is simply dismissed, not fined or imprisoned. The steward is both stunned and inspired by his master's mercy.

The dismissal is effective immediately, but the shrewd steward realizes he has a "window of opportunity" before the news reaches the renters in the village. He summons debtors and instructs them to "sit down quickly" (v. 8) and generously alters their debts.

THE MASTER'S DILEMMA

When the master discovers the steward's strategy, he faces a genuine dilemma. If he rescinds the steward's new contracts, as he is legally entitled to do because they are unlawful, he will alienate the renters and the entire village. They have already been celebrating the *master's* generosity!

If he allows these reduced contracts to stand, he will be short of produce this year, but his "honor" will spread far and wide (as also will the "honor" of the shrewd steward for arranging the deals). People will praise the noble and generous landowner.

"HAPPILY EVER AFTER"

The master applauded the shrewd steward, and everyone in this story truly lived "happily ever after." In the Mediterranean world honor is wealth. Though deprived of surplus this year, the master has gained greater honor. The steward, even though unemployed, can turn now to his former clients and make claims on them for favors as he needs them. Everyone knows that the steward "arranged" these excellent deals.

And the peasants are happy as clams. For at least this one harvest season, they might be able to live slightly above or at least just at but definitely not below the subsistence level, which is where they usually found themselves.

To the parable (vv. 1–8a), early Christians quickly added supplemental verses (8b–13), which are not easy to interpret but which relate in one or another way to shrewdness and prudence. The first application, attributed to Jesus (vv. 8b–9), is another cultural truism. The purpose of wealth or surplus is not that it be stored up in a personal retirement account (see 12:13-21) but rather that it be used in making friends. Friends, like family, are a form of social security. One can still see this value operative in the way many Middle-Eastern rulers use (or abuse) oil wealth.

Verses 10–11 redefine the steward in the parable as "unfaithful" and offer a brief reflection on Christian fidelity. Finally, verse 13 is entirely unrelated to the parable but simply summarizes a general attitude toward wealth. It ought not be allowed to distract from the worship of God. Jesus' Mediterranean lesson for Americans? Money isn't everything!

Twenty-Sixth Sunday in Ordinary Time
Luke 16:19-31

Jesus lived in a cultural world where people believed that all the goods of life (land, wealth, honor, blood, semen, etc.) were limited in quantity and already distributed. They lived by the norm "there's no more where this came from." (Contrast the American conviction "there's always more where this came from.")

To get ahead or improve one's lot in life was completely unthinkable. A person who gained something was always suspected of taking it—even if unintentionally—from someone else. This is shameful. (Both the woman who found her lost coin and the man who found his lost sheep were obliged to prove to the community that this was indeed what was lost and not something that was stolen to replace the loss.)

This background defines "rich" and "poor" in Mediterranean culture. To be rich means, among other things, that one doesn't work for a living. Zacchaeus, the "chief" of toll collectors in his region, hired collectors and levied a percentage on the toll for his support. He did not personally collect tolls.

To be poor is to have lost one's basic status, whether landowner or beggar, *temporarily.* The Bible frequently mentions poor widows and orphans in one breath—neither status is viewed as permanent.

142

THE RICH MAN AND LAZARUS

This parable contrasts a rich and poor man. The rich man is clearly affluent and blessed with surplus. His cultural obligation, common to anyone with surplus, is to give alms. Any windfall of wealth must be immediately distributed (see Luke 12:16-21). To retain surplus for oneself is to be greedy (12:15). In fact, it is perfectly appropriate to substitute "greedy" for the word "rich" in the New Testament.

Lazarus is described as a "poor man" who lay prostrate at the rich man's gate. He is probably crippled and definitely covered with sores, an impurity doubly compounded by the wild dogs who lick them.

Curiously, Lazarus is not begging. How can the rich man give alms if Lazarus is not begging? Hearers of this parable would think the worst of Lazarus: his illness suggests divine punishment. He's clearly lost his status, and by not begging he makes no effort to regain his status.

THE GATE

The gate by which Lazarus posts himself performs two functions. It keeps Lazarus outside and the rich man inside; but it can also be the rich man's entry into the world where he can give alms or become a patron to needy clients. This creates a gap between the two, which only grows larger as the story progresses.

REVERSAL OF POSITION

The theme of reversal is common in ancient stories. The surprise in this story is that only after both characters die do we learn of the reversal. Here is the first indication that the rich man was derelict.

Even in death, the rich man "still does not get it." He tries to trade on ancestral spiritual family privilege by addressing Abraham as "Father." Surely status should help, but it doesn't. Even more tactlessly, he still views Lazarus as his inferior. "Send Lazarus to refresh me!"

Abraham's response concludes the parable and makes the point. The poor one who suffered "bad things" is now consoled; the rich one who was consoled with "good things" in life is now tormented. This is not a moral teaching; it is only an illustration of the Beatitudes in Jesus' Sermon on the Plain (Luke 6:20, 24).

But as with the lost son, so in this parable there is an appendix with a stinging thrust. Here a moral dimension is introduced. The rich man's blind insistence that Lazarus be sent to warn his surviving brothers is countered with Abraham's reference to the Law and Prophets, implying that the rich man and his brothers should know about caring for the poor (see Exod 22:21-22; Deut 10:17-19; Amos 2:6-8; Jer 5:25-29).

Addressed to the Pharisees, whom Luke has parenthetically identified as "lovers of money," Jesus' parable is a message of rejection. Even if someone would return from the dead (Pharisees believed in the resurrection from the dead), the obstinate Pharisees would continue on their merry way to perdition, as did the rich man in this story.

Twenty-Seventh Sunday in Ordinary Time
Luke 17:5-10

Not long ago, Americans discovered "mentors." In general, a "mentor" helps a novice to enter or progress along a certain path toward a specific goal. In the academic world, a "mentor" guides a doctoral student through the requirements of earning a degree. In the business world, a "mentor" helps a promising person to achieve excellence, success, and often a high administrative position in a corporation.

In the Mediterranean world Jesus is not a "mentor" but rather a "faction founder" who builds his "faction" around himself by gathering "followers" or "disciples." Here is what Jesus the faction founder expects of members of his faction, often called his "disciples."

LOYALTY

The word usually translated "faith" in the New Testament is better translated as "loyalty" or "reliability." Jesus, the founder of a faction devoted to the renewal of Israel, demanded loyalty to himself and his project. Recall Jesus' expectation that, faced with a choice, a disciple should prefer him to one's family of origin (Luke 14:2, 5-26).

Luke 17 opens with a warning from Jesus about shattering the loyalty of disciples. It is not as clear here as it is in the parallels (see Mark 9:42; Matt 18:6), which speak explicitly of the little ones "who are *loyal* to me." Any disciple who breaks the loyalty of another disciple deserves to be destroyed, that is, weighed down with a millstone and cast into the sea. Frightened by Jesus' challenge, the apostles ask him to strengthen their loyalty or reliability ("increase or add to our faith," v. 5). Jesus replies that if they were even minimally loyal (had faith the size of a mustard seed), God would hear their prayer and do whatever they ask. Jesus claims that their loyalty is weak.

The connection with loyalty is clearly made in Mark's version of this incident (see 11:22-23). If disciples are loyal to God, God will move the mountain (or mulberry tree) into the sea (and cast out the demon, heal the illness, still the storm, etc.).

FORGIVENESS

The words "sin" and "forgive" in Luke 17:3-4 remind Luke's readers of Jesus' parable of the lost sons, which, having been read or heard just two chapters earlier in this Gospel, is still echoing in their minds and hearts. Disciples must be compassionate as the Father is compassionate (Luke 6:36). They must forgive as often as a sinner repents.

"DUE-NOTHING" SERVANT

In the ancient Middle-Eastern world every family, even relatively poor ones, had at least one servant. The very poorest families gave some of their children to other families as servants to ensure that they would be fed. The master in this parable apparently has only one servant who both tends the fields and does the cooking. The thrust of the story is clear and straightforward. Good servants do what they are told. A master never has to thank a servant for doing what was expected.

Most translations cause confusion with their rendition of Jesus' final advice to disciples: "When you have carried out all your orders, learn to say: we are *worthless* servants; we have only done our duty" (v. 10). "Worthless"? Is an obedient and dutiful servant really "worthless" *(New Revised*

Standard Version), or "unprofitable" (revised NT of the *New American Bible*), or "useless" *(New Jerusalem Bible),* or "good-for-nothing" (Kleist-Lilly), or "unworthy" *(RSV; New International Version)?*

Literally, the Greek adjective means "without need." The Syriac New Testament translation edited by Thomas of Harkel, bishop of Hierapolis in Syria around the years 612 and 617, rendered this adjective with an idiomatic phrase that means "owed nothing."

The *New English Bible* captures this sense in its rendition: "We are servants and *deserve no credit.*" The neologism that I propose ("due-nothing" servant) reflects the pun-oriented sense of humor that Jesus exhibited (in Aramaic) on many occasions. While this servant clearly is not a "do-nothing" person, it is also clear that a servant is "due nothing" for services rendered. Jesus' demands of forgiveness, loyalty, and the surrendering of an entitlement mentality still challenge his American disciples.

Twenty-Eighth Sunday in Ordinary Time
Luke 17:11-19

Biblical scholars and medical scientists agree that true leprosy, or Hansen's disease, almost certainly did not exist in first-century Palestine. The disease was brought to the Middle East from India by the armies of Alexander the Great about 300 B.C., but no trace of true leprosy has been found in any of the ancient bones excavated in Israel. Only one case was discovered in Egypt, and the bones were dated to the first century of the common era!

True leprosy is only mildly contagious. Even spouses do not usually "catch" it from their infected partners. Yet the scaly condition described in Leviticus 14 and 15 is feared not because it is contagious but rather because it is polluting. "Biblical leprosy" is not "catchy," it's "dirty"; and it makes individuals and the community "dirty," "impure," "unclean."

Finally, neither the Hebrew nor Greek Bible uses the correct word for "true" leprosy. Instead, the words they used describe a repulsive, flaky, or scaly condition affecting the skin, clothes, and walls of the home.

History and anthropology rather than medicine and science help us understand why our ancestors in the Faith were so concerned about this "leprosy."

LEPROSY AND BOUNDARIES

The "purity" laws in Leviticus 11–15 deal with boundaries. Leviticus 11 pertains to the mouth, an opening in the body through which "approved" and "unapproved" foods cross the body boundary and enter the interior. Leviticus 12 concerns conception and childbirth, processes that cross the body boundary through the female body opening. Leviticus 13 and 14 describe a repulsive, flaky or scaly condition affecting the skin, clothes, and walls—three kinds of boundaries. In each case the biblical text reflects the concern about whether or not the problem is deeper than the skin or, in other words, whether it has "pierced" the boundary. Finally, Leviticus 15 discusses male and female involuntary discharges or leaks escaping the body's boundaries through body openings difficult (impossible?) to control.

Anthropologists point out that a society concerned with maintaining safe and secure body boundaries is also concerned with safe and secure societal or geographical boundaries. Rules governing the physical body replicate rules governing the social or geographical body. These particular laws of Leviticus began to be vigorously enforced after the return from Babylonian Exile (587–537 B.C). In Babylon, Ezra the priest concluded that the reason God had punished the chosen people with exile was because they had married foreign, that is, non-Judaic women. They had brought "unclean" women into the boundaries of the "holy" community of Israel.

Ezra declared that, in order to restore purity and holiness to Israel, these women and their children must be dismissed immediately. On the spot, he broke the marriages and restored solid, impenetrable boundaries to Israel, making it whole and holy once more (Ezra 10; Nehemiah 9).

In this same historical period the purity laws of Leviticus 11–15 began to be rigidly enforced. Marriage laws protected the boundaries of society; purity laws protected the human body boundaries. One set of laws (purity) reflects and reinforces the other set of laws (marriage). And the reason for all these laws is to ensure that Israel would remain "holy as the Lord is holy," a recurring theme in Leviticus.

HEALING CHALLENGES BOUNDARIES

Luke reports that ten people afflicted with a repulsive, scaly skin condition (weakened body boundaries) approach Jesus and ask for *mercy* (v. 13). In the Mediterranean world, mercy describes that human quality that motivates a person to meet his or her interpersonal obligations. In effect, the ten people in Luke are asking Jesus to give them what he owes them! And what would that be?

In another instance, a leper asked Jesus "to be *made clean*" (Matt 8:1-2; Mark 1:40-45; Luke 5:12-16). Their condition posed a polluting threat to their community. They were excluded from the community and, most importantly, from common worship. They had to remain outside the boundaries. What such people are "owed" is membership in the holy community, restoration to that membership if it has been suspended. The ten who ask for mercy acknowledge that Jesus can restore them to the holy community.

Jesus as healer was constantly challenging existing boundaries and pushing them ever outward. Sinners, the blind, the lame, and lepers were welcome within the boundaries of the holy community Jesus was forming. Healing, technically, means restoring meaning to life; curing technically refers to resolving biomedical problems.

The cultural world of Jesus knew it was God alone who heals. Jesus was a gifted intermediary or broker. Nine of those healed went to Jerusalem to give "praise to God" in the presence of the priests; one came to "praise God" in Jesus' presence. Even though Jesus had not mentioned offering the sacrifice out of consideration for this Samaritan, the Samaritan knew full well he wouldn't be welcome or perhaps even permitted to enter the Jerusalem Temple. Hence he gave praise to the One who healed him and to that One's broker, Jesus. Moreover, it was only the Samaritan who said "thank you" to Jesus.

In the ancient Middle East, to say "thank you" is to end a relationship. A popular modern saying affirms, "Don't thank me; you will repay me [with a favor when I am in need]." The Samaritan recognized it would be impossible to repay his Galilean benefactor or approach him again if the problem returned, as it often did. The Judean lepers were a different story. As members of the same in-group, they could approach Jesus anywhere at any time. The Samaritan knew he was in the "wrong" place at the "right" time, and such an opportunity might never occur again for him.

The Samaritan's repulsive skin condition is ameliorated; Jesus welcomes him into the community. Other Judeans and Galileans would not be so accepting. Will we, the modern followers of Jesus, imitate our Master or his compatriots?

Twenty-Ninth Sunday in Ordinary Time
Luke 18:1-8

Cultural insights urge more precise translations of this story to show why its popular title, "The Persistent Widow," is inappropriate.

THE WIDOW

The word for "widow" in Hebrew means "silent one" or "one unable to speak." In the patriarchal Mediterranean world males alone play a public role. Women do not speak on their own behalf. A widow who has lost her husband and spokesperson to death is in an even worse condition if the eldest son is not married. Younger widows were considered to be very dangerous and were urged to remarry. One of the major concerns in the early Church was determining who truly is a widow. See the discussion in 1 Timothy 5:3-15.

Because widows were not included in Hebrew laws on inheritance, they became common symbols of the exploited and oppressed. Prophets like Isaiah (1:23; 10:2) and Malachi (3:5) criticized the harsh treatment they received, and throughout the Bible widows are viewed as being under the special protection of God (Jer 49:11; Ps 68:5; Jas 1:27).

Because the widow appears alone in this parable, we can assume that she has no male family member who can appear on her behalf. She is truly alone and therefore in a very vulnerable situation. At the same time, she is desperate. Being already deprived of everything of value in this society, what else does she have to lose? her life?

THE JUDGE

Very likely a local magistrate, this is a stock character for Luke (see 12:14, 58; Acts 18:15). A Torah-observant judge would feel obliged to take special care of the widow (see Deut 10:18; 14:29; 16:11). If nothing else, a judge might surely fear the "curse" for not doing justice for a widow (see Deut 27:19). But this judge is none of the above. The story asserts (v. 2) and the judge himself admits (v. 4) that he does not fear God and that he is "shameless," that is, no one can make him "feel ashamed."

In the cultural world of Jesus, where honor is the core value and shame is its unfailing corollary, the judge is a cultural misfit. Worse, without this basic cultural equipment he can hardly be expected to do justice. What does he care how his actions would be seen and interpreted by the community, or what their impact might be?

THE CRUNCHER

The widow "keeps coming" to the judge. Remember that this is not a private audience; it is a very public event. The entire community waits, watches, and witnesses the event regularly. What finally moves the judge is not her persistence but rather that, literally translated, "she will end up giving me a black eye" (v. 5). The Greek word in that verse is borrowed from boxing. The Greek language also used the word figuratively to mean "blacken one's face," which means to publicly shame a person. The translation "wear me down" is incorrect and misses the entire point: "shame."

By publicly badgering the judge every day, the woman repeatedly shames this shameless person. Who knows but, at some point, that she might not even poke him in the eye, literally? And the judge who boasts that he is insensitive to shaming strategies and cares not a whit about his honor ultimately yields to her pressure. After all, in a culture where law-courts were not about justice but shaming others no matter what the cost, this judge would be damaged by the gossip report that a woman has shamed him. He'd never live that down and couldn't continue as judge.

MORAL OF THE STORY

Jesus' conclusion is: If a helpless widow can get through to a shameless judge, all the more can a petitioner be heard by an honor-sensitive God. (Recall Ezek 36:16-32 as one instance where God indicates greater concern for personal honor than for the house of Israel. Others would besmirch God's reputation, and God, like any other honor-driven being, simply can't allow that to happen.)

The moral makes convincing sense in the Mediterranean world but may be less convincing in the modern world. Many believers remember offering prayers that seem to have gone unanswered. Some spiritual wags have remarked: "Of course God answered. The answer was no." This observation may be too simplistic. Remember that the Mediterranean world is strongly group oriented. The widow's petition was publicly made; for all his bluster and denial, the judge respected public opinion. It was group pressure that made the judge cave in.

Americans are individualistically oriented and generally discount the value of the group. Americans generally address individualistic prayers to God in private. No group hears, no group can help. The widow's strategy is worth pondering.

Thirtieth Sunday in Ordinary Time
Luke 18:9-14

The editor of this scene clearly identifies the focus of this parable: those who trusted in themselves as being righteous and who scorned others. In Luke's story line this is unmistakably the Pharisees and lawyers.

THE PHARISEE

If Christians know the Pharisees only from New Testament information, they are badly informed and the impression is erroneous. Precious little of the New Testament gives a fair report or interpretation of them. Pharisees were one of a number of factions in the world of Jesus. They formed a "fellowship" (*haburah* in Hebrew) whose members practiced distinctive observances of prayer, fasting, almsgiving, and tithing.

In the parable, the Pharisee's prayer is self-focused, just like Mary's Magnificat (Luke 1:46-56) and Simeon's Canticle (2:29-31). Unlike those prayers, however, the Pharisee's has an unmistakable elitist edge ("not like other people . . . especially that tax-agent," v. 10) spelled out in the details of his piety. His disclaimer ("not rapacious, unrighteous, adulterer") is falsified in Luke's story line. Jesus accuses the Pharisees of being full of rapacity (11:39), money lovers (16:14), and—implied by juxtaposition—adulterers (16:18).

Fasting. Christians (Acts 13:2-3; 14:23) and Judeans both fasted. The Judean tradition was more concerned with the public fast days (e.g., day of atonement, see Lev 16:29-31). This Pharisee boasts of going beyond the norm.

Tithing. The basic idea of tithing in Deuteronomy 14:22-29 evolved and was elaborated throughout history. Tithing took a wide variety of forms in the biblical record, and one must be careful when discussing tithing to identify very specifically the historical period of the practice under discussion. The first-century Pharisees distinguished themselves by observing a first and second tithe, that is, a very high standard beyond the legal requirements.

THE TAX AGENT

The Greek word most often translated as "publican" or "tax collector" can describe three categories of people in the first century: (1) those who purchased the right from government to collect specific taxes; (2) supervisory officials, regional directors, like Zacchaeus (a "chief" collector or agent); and (3) employees or agents who collected indirect taxes through tolls at major transport and commercial centers like Jericho and Capernaum. Members of this third category of agents were employed by higher authorities, hence the Baptist urges that they collect no more than is "appointed" (Luke 3:12-12). Someone else has set the rates. While despised and avoided by the Pharisees, tax agents formed one of the groups that responded to the prophet John and the prophet Jesus.

The tax agent in this parable presents a humble contrast to the puffed-up Pharisee. He stands far off and adopts the customary posture for prayer: arms crossed over the chest and eyes cast downward. To strike the breast is a Middle-Eastern gesture peculiar to women (Luke 23:27). Men use it only in extreme anguish, as here and likely in Luke 23:48. The tax agent simply repeats: "God have mercy on me. I am a sinner." Or as we noted about mercy above, "God give me what you owe me. Fulfill your interpersonal obligation to me. I am a sinner." The Pharisee thought he had it all sewed up, but the tax agent was the one God justified (v. 14). The Pharisee needed nothing; the tax agent recognized he needed God.

CONCLUSION

The final saying about exalting and humbling self is known as a "floating saying." It appears here and in 14:11, both stories aimed in criticism at the Pharisees. Other forms of this wisdom occur in Matt 18:4; 23:12; Jas 4:6, 10; and 1 Pet 5:6. From the cultural perspective of honor and shame, one must always guard against making a hollow claim or a claim that can be easily dismissed. Sitting in the wrong place is risky; sitting lower and being invited higher is wiser.

But the verb in this saying is in the "theological" passive voice, something quite common in the Bible. In passive-voice constructions the agent is not mentioned but can be deduced from the context. In the Bible, when no human agent is identified, the agent is then understood to be "God." Thus whoever humbles self will be exalted (by God, of course); and whoever exalts self, will be humbled (by God, of course).

In other words, this is another story of divine reversal. God's ways are not the way humans think and plan. Most people go through life and tally successes and failures. Believers sometimes can discover in their so-called failures examples of divine reversals, a better plan, a more rewarding venture. What looks initially like a set-back can be an opportunity for course correction.

Thirty-First Sunday in Ordinary Time
Luke 19:1-10

Poor Zacchaeus! So frequently has he been unfairly compared to the twentieth-century Internal Revenue Service in the United States that his reputation has been sorely tarnished. Listen again to what Mediterranean cultural insights reveal about his true character.

ZACCHAEUS THE "RICH" MAN

Economics as we know it began to develop after Adam Smith and Karl Marx. In antiquity economics and economic understanding operated at a very different level. The terms "rich" and "poor," which we use rather frequently, had quite different meanings in the ancient world than they do for us.

The people who populate the pages of our Bible believed that all things of value in life already existed, were limited in quantity, and already distributed. This included honor, semen, wealth, blood, anything else one could think of. People had whatever they had. If someone suddenly lost some good, it was suspected that someone else had gained it. The one who had suddenly gained something had to prove it was not stolen. There was no honorable way to increase one's goods.

The word "poor" therefore described people who had temporarily fallen out of their status. It was their task to resume normal status as quickly as possible. In the Bible, the poor are frequently clustered with "widows and orphans." Widows could regain their status by remarrying. The status of orphan is characteristic of childhood. One could be adopted by others or eventually grow into adulthood and marry, leaving the status of orphanhood behind.

One ancient understanding of "rich" people is those who did not have to "work for a living." Such were very powerful patrons served by clients, servants, and others who carried out their wishes. Zacchaeus the "rich" man belonged in this category. Sometimes "rich" can mean "greedy" in the Bible, but as this story progresses it will become clear that Zacchaeus does not seem to be greedy.

As a toll collector, Zacchaeus bid to Rome for the right to collect tolls, not personally but through agents. When Rome accepted his bid, Zacchaeus paid them the toll for his region in full. Then it was up to him to recoup his bid by collecting the tolls and trying to make a profit if possible. He relied on agents to do that work. Enviable as it may sound, few toll collectors managed to recoup their bid and fewer still managed to make a profit. Zacchaeus was rich in that others, hired agents, did his work for him. In his case, "rich" did not mean "greedy."

ZACCHAEUS THE "RIGHTEOUS" MAN

When Jesus invites himself to Zacchaeus' house, the Pharisees grumble that he is a "sinner." Zacchaeus defends himself quite pointedly. Indeed, he literally stopped the procession to his house to publicly demonstrate that he is not a sinner as charged.

First, he admits to giving half of his possessions to the poor. Zacchaeus uses the present tense, which in the Greek language describes repeated, customary practice. Zacchaeus does this on a regular, ongoing basis. Most translations use the future tense ("I will give"), which is grammatically possible but less plausible. In Luke, giving alms is a sign of righteousness (6:30-31, 38; 11:41; 12:33; 16:9; 18:22, 29).

Second, he pronounces a conditional clause: "IF I have cheated someone," whose form in Greek does not imply that he consciously committed extortion but only that if he discovers that he has cheated, then he has a plan whose details are truly amazing. He restores what he has inadvertently cheated fourfold (400 percent)! The Torah (see Lev 6:5 and Num 5:6-7) demanded the restoration of the object plus one-fifth (20 percent) interest. Roman law required fourfold restitution only from a convicted criminal. Zacchaeus has surpassed the Torah's requirements and met the most stringent of terms in Roman law.

THE NAME "ZACCHAEUS"

This name appears only here in the New Testament. In the Old Testament it occurs only at 2 Maccabees 10:19. The Hebrew word from which this name is formed means "clean, pure, innocent." Luke has reported the story of "Mr. Clean, Mr. Pure, Mr. Innocent," but poor Zacchaeus has unfortunately rarely been presented as such.

Scholars are divided about whether Zacchaeus "converted" on the occasion of meeting Jesus or had done so earlier in his career. I side with the scholars who claim Zacchaeus converted earlier and was misjudged by the grumbling Pharisees. Even in antiquity the only exercise some people got was jumping to conclusions.

In this interpretation of the Zacchaeus story, contemporary Western believers can find in this much-maligned character an excellent model of self-esteem. Jesus recognized his worth by calling him "Son of Abraham" rather than "Son of tax collectors." Jesus knew and publicly proclaimed Zacchaeus' true identity. With more than 75 percent of Americans suffering low self-esteem, Zacchaeus is a fine example of how to resist and survive the critical comments of others.

Thirty-Second Sunday in Ordinary Time
Luke 20:27-38

The Middle-Eastern culture of Jesus was a rough-and-tumble world. Modern-day "negative campaigning" and sharp political debates are tame in contrast.

CHALLENGE AND RIPOSTE

The honor-driven culture of the Middle East is conflict-prone at its core. To gain and augment personal honor, one must challenge another in the hope that the challenged person will make a weak riposte. (The term "riposte" comes from fencing and describes the swift thrust made after parrying an opponent's lunge. Observe Jesus' "parry" and "swift thrust" in all his arguments with opponents!)

In today's story, the conflict is between a Sadducee and Jesus. It is one of a cluster of arguments in this section of Luke. Since Jesus gives a basically Pharisaic answer to the Sadducee challenge, the story reflects typical Sadducee and Pharisee conflict.

THE CHALLENGE

The Sadducees did not believe in the resurrection because they believed only what was revealed in the *written* Torah. They totally rejected the *oral* Torah, or traditions held by the Pharisees. Since Sadducees claim that there is no reference to resurrection in the written Torah, they didn't believe in it. The hypothetical question about the woman with seven *successive* husbands is rooted in the Law of Moses, Deuteronomy 25:5-10. This Law seeks to guarantee family continuity. All kinds of disastrous consequences result if a man dies with no heir or his wife is widowed without a son. Since the ideal marriage partner is a first cousin, the brothers of the deceased man are the ideal new partners (= first cousins) for the widow. The entire pattern of thinking is family centered and this-worldly.

Those who believe in the resurrection must explain how the woman in this hypothetical case will manage seven husbands *simultaneously* in the age to come, a silly situation on its face. The challenge to Jesus is clear: do you believe in the *written* Torah, or do you side with the Pharisees, accept their belief in the resurrection based on *oral* traditions and interpretations, and subject Moses to ridicule?

THE RIPOSTE

Remember that Jesus routinely replies to opponents with an insult (e.g., "hypocrites!" or "can't you read?"). Insult follows insult in what follows. First, Jesus explains the facts of life and reproduction to mature, grown men (vv. 34–35). Immortal beings don't need to reproduce; only humans do that to ensure the continuity of the race.

The next insult is double-barreled. He tells the Sadducees that those whom God considers worthy of the age to come and worthy of resurrection are immortal, like angels. The Sadducees did not believe in angels, or spirits either (Acts 23:8)! The shot from the second barrel is that Jesus identifies these immortals as "children [literally, sons] of God," a favorite Old Testament name for angels (Gen 6:2; Job 1:6), since they share in the resurrection, a life-giving act of God.

Finally, the crowning insult. Jesus quotes the Torah against its champions, who are so committed to its literal interpretation. He argues that Moses himself proves the resurrection when he describes the Lord as "God of Abraham, Isaac, and Jacob" (v. 38). These patriarchs were long deceased by Moses' time. Since only the living can have a God, and God claims to be God of the patriarchs, God somehow sustains the patriarchs in life in the "age to come."

Luke concludes Jesus' argument with an allusion to 4 Maccabees 7:19 (dated between A.D. 18 and 55). Luke's phrase "for to God all of them are alive" reflects the belief of the pious recorded in Maccabees "that to God they do not die, as our patriarchs Abraham, Isaac, and Jacob died not, but *live to God.*"

We don't know how the Sadducees responded, but some of the scribes (who are very likely Pharisees) publicly honor Jesus for winning yet another round against formidable opponents. "Teacher, you have put it well!"

Jesus won all arguments in his life and ministry and built an honorable reputation. But his success at insult also contributed to his death. Americans tempted to exchange their culture's preference for civility for Jesus' Mediterranean hostility and offensiveness should consider all the potentially lethal consequences.

Thirty-Third Sunday in Ordinary Time
Luke 21:5-19

To read this passage with respect for and sensitivity to Mediterranean culture, an American believer needs to keep a few things in mind.

First, many scholars agree that Luke is writing his Gospel around A.D. 80 or 85. Jesus has already died, risen, and ascended. The city and Temple of Jerusalem are already destroyed. Acts of the Apostles records the difficulties experienced by believers after Jesus died. Thus the events that Jesus "foretells" in today's reading have already occurred for Luke's first readers. Putting them on Jesus' lips is how Luke enhances Jesus' reputation as someone who knows the will of God and knows the forthcoming, perhaps even the future—which would boggle the first-century Mediterranean mind.

Second, throughout his Gospel Luke presents Jesus as a "prophet mighty in word and deed" (Luke 24:19), particularly a healing prophet who preaches repentance and leads those whose lives have lost cultural meaning back to the proper purpose and direction in life. In essence, a prophet is a spokesperson for God, one who is holy or separate, and one who acts aggressively against sin. The prophet usually proclaims God's will for the here and now; the message is very present-oriented. "Repent!"

Third, Mediterranean culture is basically and primarily present-oriented. "Give us *today* our bread for today," they pray, unlike Americans who would pray for a month's or year's supply in order to get on with life. Even if one chooses the acceptable, alternate translation: "Give us today *tomorrow's* bread," the peasant vision covers a wide-ranging present but nothing more.

In today's reading Luke's Jesus affirms: "Truly, I tell you, *this generation* [the one contemporary with his ministry] will not pass away until all things have taken place" (v. 32). But that one and many additional generations have passed away, and all things still have not taken place.

Fourth, in the Mediterranean world only God knows the distant future and the distant past. Prophets know the distant future only if God has revealed it to them. The only way to know whether a prophet is authentic is when the prophecy is fulfilled (Deut 18:21).

Luke's presentation of the earthly Jesus foretelling the fall of the city and Temple of Jerusalem along with persecution of his disciples is enhanced by the fact that these have occurred and continue to occur. Because these events have come true, Jesus is judged reliable in other predictions, especially about the "coming Son of Man" (v. 27ff.).

THE "PREDICTIONS"

Jesus (around A.D. 30) predicts the Judean revolt against Rome (A.D. 66–70; v. 10). Earthquakes (v. 11) are associated with theophanies of the Lord (see Ezek 3:12-13), and famine is a common form of divine punishment (Ezek 36:29-30).

But before this revolt takes place (v. 12), Jesus' disciples will meet with violent arrest (Acts 4:3; 5:18) and will be handed over (see Acts 8:3) to prisons (Acts 5:19; 8:3) and synagogues (Acts 9:2; 26:11). His disciples will face kings (Acts 21:1; 25:13) and governors (Acts 23:24, 26) on account of Jesus' name (see Luke 6:22; 9:48; Acts 4:7, 10, 17-18).

In Acts of the Apostles, the sequel to his Gospel, Luke offers additional illustrations of the various predictions of Jesus. Both books should be read together as one unit.

CULTURAL INSIGHTS

In addition to the distinctive present-time orientation of our ancestors in the Faith, two other cultural characteristics deserve notice: family persecution (v. 16) and deception (v. 8).

Family persecution. In the turbulence stirred by the Judean revolt against Rome, Jesus' disciples who were earlier urged to "hate family" (Luke 14:26-27), leave them behind (Luke 18:29), and join Jesus' new, extended family (Luke 14:26-27) are now persecuted by those rebuffed blood relatives. Jesus himself was handed over by one of the Twelve (Luke 22:3), his fictive-kin group, for all purposes, *his* family (8:21).

Deception. Because prophecy required fulfillment in order to be authenticated, those who listened to prophets were hard pressed to tell who was truthful and who was lying (see Jer 23:9-40; 28:1-17). Many might not live long enough to witness the prophecy's fulfillment. For this reason Jesus cautions his disciples against being deceived (v. 8) by those who will prophecy in his name! Do not follow them!

The final comment is familiar if troublesome to American believers: "by your endurance you will gain possession of your lives" (v. 19). Stick it out. Offer it up. Suffer. Persevere. Take-charge Americans would want to do more! What else can they do in difficult times?

Thirty-Fourth Sunday in Ordinary Time (Christ the King)
Luke 23:35-43

Scripture scholars are fond of repeating that "the best commentary on the Bible is the Bible." (See, for example, the *New Oxford Annotated Bible with the Apocrypha, Revised Standard Version,* p. xxii, the conclusion to the section explaining the abbreviations of the books of the Bible: "The best commentary on the Bible is often some other text in the Bible . . .").

JESUS, THE SECOND ADAM

In Luke's temptation scene (4:1-13), Jesus "passes" the temptation that Adam "failed" (Genesis 3). Adam was tempted to eat forbidden fruit. He did and lost status as "son of God" (Gen 3:1-7). Jesus was tempted to turn stone into bread (4:2). He didn't and remains truly "Son of God."

Adam had dominion over all things (Gen 1:26-30) but yearned to "be like God" (Gen 1:26-30). He yielded to Satan and lost his dominion as he became subject to sin and death (Gen 2:17; 3:19). Jesus was offered power over the whole world (Luke 4:5-6) but rejected it. He remained subject only to God's will.

Adam was told that by eating the fruit he would "not die" (Gen 3:4). He obeyed Satan and died (see Gen 3:19). Jesus is tempted to defy death by jumping from the Temple, but he allowed God to remain Lord of life and death, preferring obedience to God rather than to Satan (Luke 4:12). Jesus is a welcome "second Adam."

TEMPTED ON THE CROSS

There are similarities between Jesus' new temptations on the cross and his previous temptations by Satan. Notice three challenges to Jesus by his enemies: "let him save himself" (23:35); "save yourself" (23:37); "save yourself and us" (23:39)! Like the earlier temptations, these challenges are based on Jesus' relationship to God: "If you are the Christ of God, his chosen one" (23:35). In both instances Jesus is urged to defy death: jump off the Temple and live; escape execution.

While Satan and Jesus' opponents propose that since Jesus is "Son of God," he will not die, the Lukan interpretation claims that precisely because Jesus is truly "Son of God" he *will* die in obedience to God's will. Jesus' obedience will have life-giving consequences far surpassing the death-dealing disobedience of Adam.

PARADISE

The repentant thief was promised "paradise" by Jesus. It is difficult to explain what paradise is because in first-century Judaism there were divergent opinions on everything! At best one can say that paradise belongs to a long-standing biblical expectation that "the end will be like the beginning." "Paradise" is a condensed symbol of the Genesis story, which offers guidance for dealing with sin and death. From Adam and his sin onward, "paradise" symbolizes temptation and disobedience, death, the reign of Satan, a place with locked gates.

Jesus inaugurates a new period featuring obedience to God, life, the end of Satan's reign (Luke 10:18), and reopens the gates of paradise, which now symbolizes the effects of Jesus' good deeds: renewed friendship with God.

CHRIST THE KING

Though Jesus spoke of the "reign or kingdom of God," he rejected the title of "king" and all attempts to "enthrone" him. What does today's gospel and its interpretation teach us about this culturally jarring feast of "Christ the King"?

The Franciscan Order was instrumental in establishing this feast and extending its celebration to the universal Church. The Order followed the lead of its great thirteenth-century theologians St. Bonaventure and Blessed Duns Scotus, who disagreed with Aquinas' conviction that, if Adam hadn't sinned, the Second Person of the Trinity would never have become flesh. They believed Jesus was incarnate before Adam and therefore before the sin. The Franciscans drew enlightenment from Scripture that Christ is the first-born of all creation (Col 1:15). They reasoned thus: How could God, a pure spirit, create Adam, an inspirited body, in the divine image and likeness (Gen 1:26-27)? Only by look-ing at the embodied, incarnate Jesus, who served as the model! Since God does not exist in time, God does not have past or future but only an eternal "now," an eternal present. (Humans experience the eternal present in their dreams where past and future characters and events run together into the present moment of the dream.)

This Franciscan theological position is closely linked with the Adam-Jesus parallels in the New Testament developed by Luke and others. With these historical insights as back-ground, today's feast reminds Christians that the best com-mentary on the Bible is the Bible.

Recommended Readings

Dunning, James B. *Echoing God's Word.* Arlington, Va.: The North American Forum on the Catechumenate, 1992.

Elliott, John H. *What Is Social-Scientific Criticism?* Minneapolis: Fortress Press, 1993.

Esler, Philip F. *The First Christians in Their Social Worlds: Social Scientific Approaches to New Testament Interpretation.* London: Routledge, 1994.

Johnson, Luke Timothy. *The Gospel of Luke.* Sacra Pagina, 3. Collegeville, Minn.: The Liturgical Press, 1992.

Malina, Bruce J. *Windows on the World of Jesus: Time Travel to Ancient Judea.* Louisville, Ky.: Westminster/John Knox Press, 1993.

Malina, Bruce J., and Richard L. Rohrbaugh. *Social-Science Commentary on the Synoptic Gospels.* Minneapolis, Minn.: Fortress Press, 1992.

Malina, Diane-Jacobs. *Beyond Patriarchy: The Images of Family in Jesus.* New York/Mahwah: Paulist Press, 1993.

Neyrey, Jerome H. *The Resurrection Stories.* Zacchaeus Studies: New Testament. A Michael Glazier Book. Collegeville, Minn.: The Liturgical Press, 1988.

Neyrey, Jerome H., ed. *The Social World of Luke-Acts: Models for Interpretation.* Peabody, Mass.: Hendrickson, 1991.

Oakman, Douglas E. *Jesus and the Economic Questions of His Day.* Lewiston, N.Y.: Mellen, 1986.

Pilch, Jean Peters. "Planning–Luke." *Celebration: An Ecumenical Worship Resource* 22 (1993) passim.

Pilch, John J. Praying with Luke." *The Bible Today* 18 (1980) 221–5.

_____. *Introducing the Cultural Context of the New Testament.* Hear the Word! Vol. 2. New York/Mahwah: Paulist Press, 1991.

_____. *The Triduum: Breaking Open the Scriptures of Holy Week.* Columbus, Ohio: Initiatives Publications, 1993.

_____. "Illuminating the World of Jesus Through Cultural Anthropology." *The Living Light* 31 (1994) 20–31.

_____. "The Transfiguration of Jesus: An Experience of Alternate Reality." *Modelling Early Christianity,* ed. Philip F. Esler. London: Routledge, 1995.

_____. "Jews and Christians: Anachronisms in Bible Translations." *PACE* 25 (1996)18–22.

Pilch, John J., and Bruce J. Malina, eds. *Biblical Social Values and the Meaning: A Handbook.* Peabody, Mass.: Hendrickson, 1993.

Pontifical Biblical Commission. *The Interpretation of the Bible in the Church.* Rome: Libreria Editrice Vaticana, 1993. Also in *Origins* 23:29 (January 6, 1994).